I Want to Talk With
my TEEN About

GUY STUFF

BY
DR. DAVID OLSHINE

Standard ®
P U B L I S H I N G
Bringing The Word to Life
Cincinnati, Ohio

Credits

Credits
Produced by Susan Lingo Books™
Cover by Diana Walters

13 12 11 10 09 08 07 06   9 8 7 6 5 4 3 2 1
0-7847-1894-6

Contents

Introduction

Why talk to your son about guy stuff?

The past few years have produced an onslaught of books and magazines for guys, focusing on sports, hunting, athletics, muscle building, motorcycles—and girls! It dawned on me that we are in a "male" crisis, with few knowing how to take our sons into something other than athletics and watching TV.

Adolescence is the period between childhood and adulthood. Some have defined this turbulent time as a season of growth to maturity. But with so much focus on outside hobbies, sports, and muscle-building, we begin to wonder if guys are growing up mature and if they're destined to do anything significant with their lives. With these worries in mind, *how* do parents guide their teen sons through this turbulent season of transition?

Guys are complex. They are wired in dramatically different ways than girls. How do guys think differently than girls? How do they act differently? Are there any stereotypes about guys that are true? Are all guys masculine and all girls feminine, and what exactly does that mean? How does faith help mature teen guys into godly men who make a difference in the world?

It's tough being a guy today. It's also tough being a parent of a teenage guy. There are few solid road maps to keep us going in the right direction. That's why we need help. Our culture hasn't quite figured it out, nor have the schools, the government, or faith-based institutions. It's imperative we go to a more reliable source for solid footing—God's Word! Armed with God's wisdom and leaning on those who have gone before us, we can make progress in growing young boys into *real* men who respect others, serve God, and make a difference in our world. Now, let's talk about guy stuff!

David Olshine

Where Do You Stand?

Walking alongside your son as he moves through adolescence is difficult, exciting, and confusing—all at the same time! The following questionnaire will help you evaluate your own strengths and weaknesses and where your own values and philosophies fit in. Circle the number that best corresponds to your answer. Then add up the total of your answers and check out the How You Scored box! (Retake the quiz after reading the book to see if your score changed!)

OPTIONS

❶ Strongly agree

❷ Agree somewhat

❸ Disagree somewhat

❹ Strongly disagree

I FEEL SECURE IN MY OWN ROLE AS A PARENT—AND NOT JUST IN BEING A FRIEND.

❶   ❷   ❸   ❹

I REGULARLY TALK WITH MY SON ABOUT HIS WORLD, THOUGHTS, AND DREAMS.

❶   ❷   ❸   ❹

I FEEL THAT RESPECTING OTHERS AND PUTTING THEM FIRST IS ONE OF THE MOST IMPORTANT THINGS WE CAN DO IN LIFE.

❶   ❷   ❸   ❹

I ENCOURAGE MY SON TO INVITE HIS FRIENDS OVER SO I CAN GET TO KNOW WHO HE ENJOYS BEING WITH.

❶   ❷   ❸   ❹

IN OUR FAMILY, CONSEQUENCES ARE IMPLEMENTED WHEN GUIDELINES ARE BROKEN.

❶ ❷ ❸ ❹

I FEEL COMFORTABLE INITIATING DISCUSSIONS WITH MY TEEN ABOUT SEX, DATING, OR RELATIONSHIPS.

❶ ❷ ❸ ❹

I ALWAYS TRY TO TEACH MY TEEN ABOUT RESPECTING WOMEN, VALUING OTHERS, HUMILITY, AND FAITH.

❶ ❷ ❸ ❹

I HANDLE CONFLICTS WITH FAMILY MEMBERS, FRIENDS, AND CO-WORKERS IN HEALTHY WAYS, CONTROLLING MY ANGER.

❶ ❷ ❸ ❹

I ENCOURAGE MY SON TO SEEK OUT WAYS TO SERVE AT CHURCH OR IN THE COMMUNITY.

❶ ❷ ❸ ❹

I LET MY SON KNOW WHEN I AM PROUD OF HIM—AND EXPRESS IT REGULARLY.

❶ ❷ ❸ ❹

HOW YOU SCORED

10—20 Give yourself a pat on the back! You have an honest perspective on yourself and are intentional about helping your son do the same. You take your role as a parent seriously and spend time investing in your son. As he watches you, he will have a tangible model of a godly person.

21—31 Your perspective on the issues your son faces may need a bit of refocusing. You want to discuss tough topics but may find yourself feeling uncertain in the world of today's teen guys. Be encouraged, knowing that as you invest in your own self-esteem, relationships, and conflict resolution, the result will be reflected in your relationship with your son as well.

32—40 Perhaps you're still struggling with where you fit in. You long to invest in your son so he can develop into a healthy, God-fearing, respectful young man, but you may be overwhelmed. Start with small steps and pray for God's leading. Your son will thank you!

The Gift of Gender

It seems everyone is trying to figure out guys. Parents are, and so are girls. What does it mean to be a guy? Who are we anyway? Who are we supposed to be, and what are we called to do with our lives? And why is the concept of "dirt" important as we build boys into men?

God made us in his image.

Genesis 2:7 tells how God created man from dust and blew life into him. God named his first human creation Adam, "land" or "dirt," to represent where man came from. But although guys were formed from dust, they were also created uniquely in God's image.

Individuality is a gift.

Genesis 1:26-28 relates how God made man in his image so he could care for creation as he subdued it. Adam was given the job of maintaining the Garden of Eden and naming the animals. So what was God doing with Adam during this time? Adam was being shaped and allowed to forge his unique identity. In other words, Adam was establishing his individuality.

key point
CELEBRATE YOUR SON'S UNIQUE GIFTS.

Guys today are no different from Adam. Just as Adam discovered who he was, the primary task for adolescent guys today is figuring out who they are. It's a battle for individuality, autonomy, and identity. They struggle with many personal choices: *Do I follow my friends or obey my parents? Do I develop my own system of beliefs and values? Who am I?* And just as important, *Who do I belong to?*

Your son is fearfully and wonderfully made. He was created with potential out of this orbit! Your job isn't to do everything for him but to facilitate an atmosphere of learning. You are a coach or consultant. Draw your son out; allow him to experience life. Guys are wired to work, manage, and lead. Most males don't enjoy being passive. We are active, love adventure, and desire to explore our individuality.

7 WAYS TO ENCOURAGE INDIVIDUALITY

- Explore new things together.
- Support and encourage new ideas.
- Avoid living vicariously through your child.
- Promote "win and grow" attitudes—not "win or lose!"
- Provide structure and security.
- Encourage dreams, hopes, and aspirations.
- Express thanks to God for individuality.

"Genesis" means new beginnings.

❖ How is your son's journey from teen to adult a form of "genesis"?

❖ What made the journey easier for you? harder?

❖ How can the gift of individuality make the trip easier for your son?

Guys like to figure things out for themselves. A boy will wrestle with questions such as: *What does it mean to be a man? What does success look like? What values and beliefs do I embrace or reject?* This is the act of "naming" or identifying important issues. Adam named the animals. Your son will come to name his issues: insecurities, popularity, masculinity, hope, humility, courage, fear, and a thousand others. And as an individual, he will arrive at many answers.

Gender is a gift from God.

Guys and girls didn't just happen. God *planned* for our genders—and he saw that they were good. Genesis 1:27 tells us that *"God created man in his own image, in the image of God he created him; male and female he created them."* From the beginning, God has celebrated gender. While his other parts of creation were "good," God looked at humans— male and female— and declared it "very good." Our gender is a gift from God, and so are the differences between the genders. If God had wanted only one gender, he wouldn't have created two!

> **key point**
> **BOTH GENDERS ARE EQUALLY IMPORTANT!**

POINTS TO PONDER...

- How do I talk about the opposite gender?
- What do I value about my own gender?
- How can I help my teen son recognize the value in *both* girls and guys?
- Do I ever play favorites between guys and girls (or my son and daughter)? When and why?

God doesn't play favorites—and neither should parents! Avoid falling into the comparison trap and celebrate the gifts and talents of all your kids!

These days it's not unusual to find competition between the genders. Are guys or girls smarter? Which gender is more focused on school or performs better on SAT tests or driver's exams? The questions and comparisons rage on—but here is the big question: *Does it matter?* Of course not! God created *both* genders with awesome gifts and talents!

BIG BIBLE POINT

Read aloud Genesis 2:7, 15 with your teen. Then discuss the following questions:

❖ Why was making man part of God's plan?

❖ What plans did God have for man?

❖ What gifts did God give to man?

❖ How can our gender and work honor God?

key point

HORMONES MAKE BOYS RISK TAKERS.

Experts have observed that from infancy on, boys are more aggressive than girls and have a more vigorous motor-activity level than girls. Boys hit more and tend to be more competitive and aggressive than girls. What's the prime cause of this gender difference? Testosterone! The differences between men and women (remember the Venus and Mars books?) are many. Guys' brains work differently than girls' do. Guys feel and think in different ways than girls do. And each "wiring" is a gift from God.

A teenage boy is a warrior who wants to fight, win, and conquer. He loves a challenge and generally wants victory at any cost. The David and Goliath story is loved by most guys because they thrive on conquering whatever "giant" they are facing. Youth leader Rick Bundschuh refers to some teenage guys as stallions: hard to tame, wild, unpredictable, and dangerous. These kids may be troublemakers or strong leaders who are just going in the wrong direction. If so, we need to help guide their energy and creativity in a "profitable direction" (*Passed Thru Fire*).

Headstrong, strong-willed, or a strong leader? Each can be used by God—given the right guidance!

11

Men and women react differently.

Boys and girls are radically different, which is a wonderful miracle. The world would be really boring if God had made both genders the same. We live, love, think, dream, work, respond, process, and react in different ways.

Men think differently than women.

Brain-development theorists explain that at the start of puberty, the male brain will have a testosterone level increase of ten to twenty times more than adolescent females. This creates a desire in guys to get "whatever" fast and furiously (eating, computer games, sex, and so on), to attempt problem solving quickly and impulsively, and to discover ways to build physical tension and then release it (like sports). The nature of the teenage guy's brain is to turn on, then quickly turn off. The processing is short and speedy, and a guy's brain power turns off much sooner than a girl's. But that's not to say that girls are smart and guys are dumb—not at all!

Because teen boys tend to be oriented toward the left hemisphere of the brain, they may outperform girls in math. Females lean toward the right side, which is the function of verbal and communication skills. That's why guys may grunt and act out with video games, while teen girls talk on their phones about boyfriend problems. The male brain is more into "doing," while girls are more into "saying."

LEFT hemisphere:	RIGHT hemisphere:
logic	intuition
mathematics	feelings
categorizing	sensitivity
rationality	daydreaming
reasoning	spatial concepts
abstractions	visualizing
sequencing	creativity
rules	color

Boys are more space-oriented than girls, which means that guys don't like being confined. Their brains dictate and scream for more space. Maybe that's why hunting, fishing, and paintball are invigorating to males. Guys like figuring out how to survive and thrive in a world of big space. Girls' brains drive them toward playing imaginative games and crafts and creative role-playing like dolls or playing house. Girls are stronger at sensory data, including, taste, touch, sound, sight, and smell. Boys have more difficulty in school than girls. They don't read as much and would rather be in open spaces to explore.

> Eve was created within the lush beauty of Eden's garden. But Adam, if you remember, was created outside the garden, in the wilderness.
> —John Eldredge

Though there are many differences, men and women are alike in many ways as well. Consider the men and women who rushed to rescue the people trapped in the World Trade Centers on September 11, 2001. Both men *and* women alike took risks, showed great courage, and served in heroic ways that day! We may have tendencies toward gender-specific reactions, but qualities such as honor and courage transcend even the lines of gender!

Think back to when you were in middle school. What were you like — a "nerd" or a "jock?" Chances are you were a changing person all the time. Don't label or box your son into a certain type. Think out of the box!

Men react differently than women.

There is massive confusion on how guys and girls "feel." The stereotype is that men are analytical and women emotional. The Kiersey-Bates (also known as the Myers-Briggs) temperament inventory analyzes how thinkers and feelers make decisions. *Feelers* make decisions based on hunches and intuitions—what their gut tells them. *Thinkers* decide, not by the heart, but by the head, utilizing logic and analyzing issues. In this inventory, men lean toward the *Thinker* and women to the *Feeler*.

Is your son a Thinker or a Feeler?

key point
GUYS LIKE TO PROBLEM SOLVE.

key point
PROCESSING FEELINGS CAN BE SLOW.

Males tend to be problem solvers, so when there is a conflict with a teenage boy, chances are he will react in one of two ways: *blow up* or *clam up*. It's not surprising in a blow-up scenario to hear a door slam or expletives shouted. The clam up, however, happens more subtly: the adolescent boy silently processes a homework problem or a girlfriend's rejection for days or weeks, then comes clean when mom or dad detects that something is "not quite right." This is the outworking of his *Thinker* side. A guy who is wired as a *Feeler* will process his situation more quickly than the *Thinker*.

HOW ARE GUYS AND GIRLS DIFFERENT?

"Maturity levels."—Kristen

"Back hair!"—Baca

"Guys go solo but girls go in groups to the bathroom."—AJ

"Girls dress up; we just wear clothes."—Brian

"Girls take forever to get over stuff."—Timothy

"Guys are more competitive."—Travis

"Girls like to shop."—Paul

Boys don't usually process feelings as quickly as girls. Some use this slow processing to become cave-like and disappear from the home front of relationships to hide and recoup. Sometimes teen guys take a while to figure out if there's even something wrong with them! Give the male time to ponder his situation. Remember that guys tend to be problem solvers who want to discover meaning for themselves.

key point
BE PATIENT WITH A GUY'S SILENCE.

Guys tend to get resentful when we push the "How are you feeling?" button. With increased anxiety and tension, a guy will tend to get angry instead of crying. Crying might happen privately, but public tears for a guy is against the cultural norm. "Big boys don't cry" has been a mantra for centuries. American boys don't feel safe crying, but they do feel entitled to yell, hit, or dominate. Is it any wonder that athletics provides a safety net and outlet for the male world?

The onset of puberty brings incredible changes to the physical, emotional, and social development of middle-school guys that may affect how they react to others. Here are a few of those changes:

Physical *muscle growth; emergence of acne; aware of the opposite sex; awkwardness and clumsiness; self-absorbed; aware of outer appearance*

Emotional *lots of highs and lows; emotions can be out of control; struggles with self-worth*

Social *concerned about popularity; friendships matter more than ever; autonomy kicks in strong; a time of experimentation*

Both genders are part of God's plan.

Consider how God planned for both genders and gave each one unique gifts, abilities, and functions. Intellectually, guys and girls have some common wiring. But starting in middle school, guys and girls begin a transition from concrete to abstract thinking. Both genders will raise questions they've never asked before, such as: *Who am I? Why am I jealous of that person? Why can't I do anything well?* The intuitive side begins to check in at middle school.

> **key point**
> **BOTH GENDERS ARE IN GOD'S PLAN.**

In general, guys speak less than girls. Some studies suggest that guys say about 3,000 words a day, whereas girls speak an average of 20,000 words a day.

Both genders are idealistic, living with a "law and order" system of justice and wanting life to be fair. When something bad happens, most teens will raise questions related to faith. They may not articulate this, but they'll certainly think about it for long periods of time. Because of the teens' innocence, lack of emotional maturity, and life experience, neither gender can lean on much data from the present to the past. They just can't make sense of why grandma died suddenly. Most boys will be quiet and perhaps enter into a fantasy world of games or computers to ease their pain. Girls, on the other hand, tend to talk through their feelings.

Guys and girls learn differently. Guys learn in a visual manner and are kinesthetic— they like to "do." Girls tend to learn through listening, dialoguing, and taking notes.

Girls are more intuitive than guys. Boys want to compete; girls want to connect. Guys want to build, then tear down; girls want to relate and process and ponder. Guys don't live in the world of words, as girls tend to do.

BIG BIBLE POINT

Guys love to "do." Discuss how these Bible guys were wired to "do."

- ❖ **Noah** (built the ark)
- ❖ **Moses** (led God's people)
- ❖ **Nehemiah** (rebuilt broken walls)
- ❖ **Jesus** (died for our sins)
- ❖ **Paul** (preached to hostile crowds)

GUYS ARE PASSIONATE ABOUT SPORTS, GIRLS— LIFE IN GENERAL!

Girls tend to be driven by self-worth. They connect on a more relational level than boys usually do. Guys tend to be driven by passion, whether it's a game, a girl, a TV show, or a challenge. At middle school, both genders no longer accept pat answers as they did in elementary school. They begin to question their beliefs and system of values. They want real answers to real problems! Teen guys and girls begin to connect the dots: *the choices I make do count.* In high school, they start to see that their decisions not only make a difference today but also affect outcomes for the future.

DID YOU KNOW ...

Researchers have found that male infants are actually more emotionally expressive than female babies. But by the time boys reach elementary school, much of the emotional expressiveness has been lost or gone underground (from *Real Boys,* by William Pollack).

Both genders are equal in God's eyes.

key point
GOD CREATED MEN AND WOMEN EQUAL.

Males are not superior to females. Females are not superior to males. Both genders are on the same playing field, and equality is the name of the game. Some might want to think that, because Adam was created first, men are better than women—but of course, this isn't so. God put Adam into a deep sleep and removed one of his ribs to make woman. And when Adam saw Eve, he may have said, "Wo…Man!"

key point
BOTH GENDERS HAVE MANY GIFTS!

BIG BIBLE POINT

Share 1 Corinthians 11:11 with your teen, then discuss how God planned for blessings, warnings, and eternal life to be given to both men and women equally and how men and women complement one another.

One author has stated that men are from Mars and women from Venus. But men and women are from *God*—and have equal status in his kingdom. Eve was created because Adam was alone, his life incomplete; according to God, this was "not good." Women complement men. Without them, we'd be more of a mess. Sure, there are always exceptions to the rule. We know many girls who love outdoor wilderness trips and backpacking, and we know boys who would rather sit on the couch watching TV or cook in the kitchen. Isn't it great that God gave both females and males interests, talents, and positive qualities?

"When a man meets the mountains, he comes home. Boys are ultimately never happy at home."
—*John Muir*

Both males and females are special and unique. Men want to be in battle and fight for someone. Girls want to be in a different kind of battle—they want to be fought for. In the heart of every male is the desire to be victorious and triumphant, to win the war, and to take the princess with him. He wants to win. She wants to be won. She wants to be fought for with a vengeance.

TARGET MOMENT

Make a list of qualities God desires both genders to develop in their lives. Remind your son that God created men and women equal; both are part of his plan!

4 DEVELOPMENTAL TASKS FOR BOTH GUYS AND GIRLS

AUTONOMY

IDENTITY

INTIMACY

MORALITY

Guys and girls are equal in God's eyes but are radically different in nature!

There are four developmental tasks both genders will explore equally in their second decades of life: *autonomy, identity, intimacy,* and *morality.* All teens become more independent and autonomous, desiring privacy and asking more questions and challenging traditions. Both guys and girls search for intimacy through friendships, which is the glue of teen culture. Finally, morality becomes an issue when teens begin to search for what they believe in and why. They've been riding your faith "coattails" and now question whether they believe in God, believe in *your* God, and where boundaries lie.

Guys go through rites of passage.

Our culture doesn't consider the words *godly* and *men* in the same sentence. In fact, the church community has missed the ways and means of raising young boys into godly men. Is the phrase "godly guys" an oxymoron? What does a godly guy look like, and how do rites of passage enter in?

Jesus had his own rites of passage.

In Jesus' day, education was huge! Jewish males were reading and memorizing the Torah (the first five books of the Old Testament) at an early age. One sage was quoted as saying, *"By the age of six, we will stuff them [males] with Torah like an ox."* By 14, most Jewish boys had memorized the Torah and all of Psalms and Proverbs. By 18, many had memorized the entire Old Testament! Being a teacher of God's Word—a "rabbi"—was one of the highest honors and privileges a boy could attain.

key point
BOYS ARE IN TRANSITION.

The making of a boy into a man was a process that included markers and symbols along the way. These markers were called "rites of passages." At age 13, a Jewish male went through a ceremony called a "bar mitzvah," which was one's entry into adulthood.

Luke 2:42-52 records when Jesus went with his parents to the Feast of Passover. Going to the festival was certainly a rite of passage for Jesus—and a sign of great things to come!

In Jesus' day, strength was, first and foremost, internal—not external.

The custom in Jesus' day was for a male son to go home with one of his parents in a caravan after the festival, but something went wrong that day. Mary thought Jesus was with Joseph and vice versa. But Jesus was in the temple, sitting among the rabbis and listening to them. Jesus asked questions, and the elders were impressed with the wisdom in his answers. Jesus had made a rite of passage from a boy who loved God to a man who sought God and his wisdom!

Guys transitioning into adulthood may typically ask themselves questions such as: *Who am I? Where do I belong? Do my decisions really matter?*

TAKE 5

❶ What were your own rites of passage?

❷ What rites of passage will move your son into adulthood?

❸ How did knowing God help you grow into an adult?

❹ What would it take to elevate your son's love for Scripture?

❺ How can you help your son know God better?

Internal strength comes from developing a relationship with God. God is the author of strength, and reading, listening to, and applying God's Word will give a boy inspiration to be great on the inside. Character, courage, and seeking God are just a few of the many traits of the inside stuff that turns boys into godly men. These qualities come from transitioning your son through his own rites of passage and teaching him to love God's Word.

Rites of passage strengthen boys.

key point

CHOOSE HEALTHY RITES OF PASSAGE.

Michael Gurian writes that boys are: *"Significantly more likely to die at the hands of their caregivers ... are four times more likely than adolescent females to commit suicide ... are twice as likely as adolescent girls to be diagnosed as learning disabled ... drop out of high school at four times the rate of adolescent females."* He says further that 90 percent of adolescents who get into trouble at school are male and that the majority of adolescent alcoholics and drug users are male.

We have our work cut out for us when we take these words to heart. Our sons need a rite of passage—something larger than themselves, some passage that they can sink their teeth into. A rite of passage is a ritual or marker that moves a person to a new stage of life. Wedding ceremonies and funerals are markers or rites of passage. A rite of passage can help move a teenage boy to more confidence on the outside as he becomes a man.

Learning to drive is a rite of passage for most TEENS!

Does our society or the church have any rites of passage for adolescent boys? Some say puberty is a natural rite, while others suggest a first kiss or sexual encounter. What about a driver's license or first job? We need to help our sons find individually driven rites of passage to lead them strongly into adulthood.

"Most children never know when they become adults."
—*Wayne Rice*

AGES OF PUBERTY IN THE U.S.

14.5 YEARS		
	13 YEARS	
		11.7 YEARS
PRE-1900	1900-1970	1971-2005

From *Hurt*, by Chap Clark (2005)

Individual markers are set up by parents. Teens are in transition from childhood to adulthood. A rite of passage helps cement for your son that he is now "a man." A number of books mentioned in the More Resources section of this book encourage parents to celebrate their son's move into adulthood with a meaningful ceremony.

Consider this list of modern-day rites of passage. Which would be most helpful and which would be hurtful?

Buying a car	Getting a tattoo
Opening a checking account	Smoking or chewing tobacco
Getting a job	Going on a missions trip
Joining a gang	Drinking alcohol
Leading at youth group	Getting a body piercing
Seeing an R-rated movie	Joining a church

Becoming a godly man takes a lifetime!

TREES TAKE YEARS TO MATURE—SO DO PEOPLE!

Remember two words: *process* and *progress*. Gardeners teach us that it takes time to grow a tree. Maturation doesn't happen overnight. And for a guy who wishes to be godly, it takes a lifetime of "becoming" to be like Christ. *Becoming* is a process word. It takes years to go from a toddler to a teen, from a teen to a young adult, from a young adult to midlife. Growth and maturation— physically, mentally, and spiritually—take time.

> **key point**
> **BECOMING GODLY IS A PROCESS.**

There is never a day when someone can say, "Okay, I have arrived at being godly." Becoming the person God desires a guy to be is a process, not just a destination! The question is: *What does godly look like?*

BEING GODLY DOESN'T MEAN...
- Being at church each time the doors are open.
- Reading the Bible for hours at a time or learning every verse.
- Just being a nice guy!

> **key point**
> **PATIENCE IS WELL REWARDED IN OUR SONS!**

Boys want a cause, but when does a teen guy "get" this attribute? Courage, integrity, purity, and godliness don't just pop up one day at age 18. It's usually a series of events—highs and lows, blessings and curses—that lead a teen to desire godly qualities.

BIG BIBLE POINT

Share I Timothy 4:7-16 with your teen, then discuss the following:
a. What myths exist about teens today? what stereotypes?
b. What do you think a godly teen looks like today?
c. What does this passage teach about being young?

Flowers and plants need help from sun, water, and other nutrients to survive and thrive. This is also true for adolescent males. They will never become godly without outside influences such as parents, strong peers, a mission, and a mentor to nourish them. Parents are still the number one influence on teens. We shape their personalities and values. Extended family is next, then other caring adults and friends. Remember that becoming godly is a process that takes a lifetime to achieve!

"Every warrior gathers under a flag. The flag represents the cause and becomes the rallying point for heroes. It becomes the place where real manhood is discovered and developed."
—Rick Bundschuh

3 KEY TEEN INFLUENCES

PARENTS: Impart faith; model godliness; motivate their sons to seek God

PEERS: Influence behavior and beliefs; impart strength and conviction

MENTORS: Offer wisdom & listening; impart godly advice; challenge teens to "go deeper" spiritually

Teens are impacted and empowered by godly peers who are the glue of life for adolescents!

Qualities of a Godly Man

When people go grocery shopping for fruit, you see them thumping watermelons and tapping cantaloupes. What are they doing? They're looking for the right fruit to take home and consume. What "good fruit" or qualities should we look for in a man growing in spirit and love with God?

A clean body, mind, and heart are vital.

God made us to be complete people—not just a head or a body or simply a brain. We're three-dimensional and made whole between body, mind, and heart—and God desires us to develop boys into men who lead with their whole being. But what does this complete kind of man look like?

Real men use deodorant!

At puberty, changes happen!

When puberty hits a teen boy, many biological and chemical reactions occur within his body. The second decade for your son will bring about amazing bodily changes. Growth happens! Everything grows on the adolescent male: armpit and pubic hairs emerge, muscles strengthen, height and weight increase—the whole works!

key point
BE SENSITIVE TO CHANGES IN YOUR TEEN SON!

key point
GIRLS LIKE CLEAN-SMELLING GUYS!

It's not unusual to encounter voice changes, pimples, and smelly pits! Simply walk into a middle-school locker room! There's a verse in the Bible referring to Lazarus being dead over three days. "He stinketh!" That is the deal with adolescent boys. Puberty creates chemical imbalances, and the result is perspiration and body odor. Let your son know he can either repel girls with body odor or attract them with deodorant and a bit of cologne. Boys need to be conscious of showering and washing their faces, since chicks don't dig zits—or body odor!

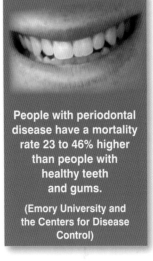

People with periodontal disease have a mortality rate 23 to 46% higher than people with healthy teeth and gums.

(Emory University and the Centers for Disease Control)

Sadly, many teens are caught up in substance abuse today. Discuss this health problem with your teen by asking, "Why would anyone intentionally do something to harm his body and not be in control of his actions?"

Acne is no fun! If it gets bad, take your son to a dermatologist. Even though God looks at the heart, he wants us to be our best in *every* aspect of our lives. And good hygiene with clear skin helps guys feel more confident. God tells us that our bodies are his temple, so we want to care for our bodies. That includes eating right, getting enough sleep, careful grooming, and avoiding substances that hurt the temple. God *does* care about our bodies, so encourage your son to make healthy choices for his body.

Help your teen realize that being clean and healthy are choices we make every day—and ones that affect our lives and relationships!

Purity reflects a clean heart and mind.

key point
PURITY BEGINS WITH FOLLOWING JESUS.

In Genesis, there were rivers flowing out of the Garden of Eden. In order to get to the Promised Land, the Israelites had to cross the Jordan River. In the last book of the Bible, Revelation 22 states that there will be a river flowing out from the throne of God. Rivers give life.

key point
OUR WALK WITH GOD STRENGTHENS PURITY.

There are a number of "rivers" we jump into during our lifetimes. One of these rivers is purity. Purity is a state of the heart and mind, a desire to be like Jesus. Purity starts with recognizing that guys are not pure but, in fact, sinful as all humans. We are fallen, broken, and in need of mending. Christ came to set us free. The river Jesus is the life-giving flow allowing us to become pure.

TAKE 5

* What does our culture think about boys?
* What do you expect from your own son?
* What do teen guys long for in life?
* How does purity affect your life?
* How can you guide your son to walk closer with God?

In our culture, many boys are made to think that following Jesus is a sissy thing, but that couldn't be further from the truth! The first step in becoming pure is to start a relationship with the only one who lived a pure life—Jesus Christ. When a relationship with Jesus takes off, it starts a series of lifelong movements. The relationship becomes established. Communication deepens. Times of wrestling with God occur, then a time of confusion, trials, errors, mountaintops, and valleys.

Teen guys need to realize that the journey toward purity with God is a *process*—a process of learning to know God's heart, mind, and will. Traveling with God isn't about speed; it's about distance—and the river of transformation can be very slow moving. Remind your teen that, since we weren't born with pure thoughts or clean hearts, the journey to purity will no doubt be a challenge. And it won't happen overnight.

WHAT DOES YOUR SON THINK?

Being pure in thought and deed isn't always easy. Where does your son stand on issues that may affect his faith and purity?

- YOU & YOUR FAMILY
- FAITH & GOD
- DRINKING & DRUGS
- HOMOSEXUALITY
- HONESTY
- LOVE & GIRLS
- MATERIALISM
- PREMARITAL SEX
- ABORTION

This journey of change involves learning to think like Jesus, act like Jesus, do everything like Jesus. The student becomes like the teacher, the mentored like his mentor. The adolescent boy is challenged to be "covered in the dust of his rabbi." This river is called *community*, which means helping your son get connected with strong peers, older college students, and others who desire to help him grow into the person God wants him to be.

Respect reflects honor to others.

The Torah (the first five books of the Bible) focuses on two areas of life: *respect for God* (loving the Lord your God) and *respect for others* (loving your neighbor as yourself). Words like *honor* and *respect* are rarely used these days. What does it mean to respect someone, and why is it important for our sons to show respect?

Respecting means giving up control.

One of the most difficult parenting responsibilities is training our kids to be respectful. Since disrespect seems to be the rule rather than the exception in today's

culture, teaching respect is like a salmon swimming upstream! The law of modern respect, according to psychologists Cloud and Townsend, states that "I'm not the only one who matters."

The hardest life lesson in learning respect might be giving up control. Refusing to comply with standards is disrespectful. Lying, stealing, and cheating are disrespectful and show a lack of self-control. There will be times when consequences need to be carried through when your son shows a disregard for your authority and a lack of control that leads to disrespect.

Who Said It?

"*Youth today love luxury. They have bad manners, contempt for authority, no respect for older people, and talk nonsense when they should be working. Young people do not stand up any longer when adults enter the room. They contradict their parents, talk too much in company, guzzle their food, lay their legs on the table and tyrannize their elders.*" — *Socrates, 500 B.C.*

At the same time, don't freak out when your son says, "You're stupid," "You don't know what you're talking about," or "I hate you." Our teens know how to push buttons and will say things that hurt and anger us at times. If you want your son to gain respect for you, his teacher, his coaches, and his friends, you must model respect for him, your spouse, and others. Adolescent respect is usually immaturity mixed with emotions and spontaneous impulses. The key is your relationship with your son. If parents choose to have lots of rules and punishments without developing a relationship, their son will push them away and cross the lines of disrespect.

> **Work at building a healthy, respectful relationship between you and your son every day!**

Parents: Ask Yourselves...

1. What is my listening style?

2. What keeps me from being a better listener?

3. How can I help my son express what he's feeling?

4. Is our communication encouraging or degrading?

5. How can I communicate better with my son?

Respect your teen's opinions even if you don't agree with them. Do you give your son freedom of speech, encouraging him to say what he thinks and feels? An open, honest family will model what respect is and is not. Don't get worked up over respect as much as obeying and behavior, says author Tim Smith. As you focus on "honor your mother and father," expect eyes to roll and arguments to abound. Through love (sometimes tough love), consequences, and trust, your son will come around.

If you want to earn respect and the right to be heard by your son, try these two time-tested principles:

- *Listen* in a way that encourages your son to *talk*.

- *Talk* without lecturing so your son will *listen*.

Treat women with respect—not as objects.

If we want to teach respect, we must understand how Jesus treated people. He valued and treated all people with dignity and grace whether they were men, women, or children. He was fair, respectful, and compassionate with all. Jesus lived in a culture that frowned on a rabbi approaching a woman in public, yet Jesus spoke with and healed women who were needy or sick. In fact, Jesus broke all cultural mores and roles by speaking with the woman of Samaria (John 4:7-26). Jesus did not care what color, creed, or religious tradition one embraced; he cared for people and respected each one.

> **key point**
> **JESUS TAUGHT US TO RESPECT ALL PEOPLE.**

Show **proper respect** to **everyone** (1 Peter 2:17).

Most teen guys enjoy helping a girl with her coat, opening doors for her, or showing respect in other ways. Remind your son that girls and women respect guys who treat them with respect!

> **key point**
> **RESPECT CROSSES ALL AGES AND GENDERS!**

Not only did Jesus speak with the Samaritan woman, but he demonstrated his respect and compassion for other women, including healing the woman who was hemorrhaging (Luke 8:43-48) and forgiving a woman caught in adultery (John 8:1-11). Jesus never treated men or women as second-class citizens—he respected them all, just as he desires us to do.

Real guys respect girls and women. Scripture calls for men to respect women, for husbands to honor their wives, and for all to serve widows. Likewise, women are called to respect men. The most important things you can teach your son about respect is that it crosses all age and gender boundaries—and that showing respect shows self-respect and honor to God.

Some guys inadvertently treat girls as if they are "less than" guys. Remind your son that objectifying girls dishonors themselves and God. Remember: God made both genders and made them without favorites!

"When men and women are able to respect and accept their differences, then love has a chance to blossom."
—John Gray

Authors Tim Sanford and Tim Geare in *Growing Pains: Advice for Parents of Teens* cite these five disrespecters of girls and women...

Challenge your son to respect the opposite sex—not as objects but as people created in the image of God. Both men and women have gifts to use in serving God. Throughout the Bible, we read about ways God used both men and women to bravely accomplish his will. We need each other, and that's why God created us to live in community with one another. Help your son recognize that it's a sign of low self-esteem to put down or treat females as objects, just as it would be for women to objectify men. We're *both* here for one reason—to glorify God and serve one another with respect!

FEMALES ARE LESS THAN HUMAN.

FEMALES ARE "SPORT."

FEMALES ARE GUYS' PROPERTY.

FEMALES' VALUE IS IN THEIR APPEARANCE.

FEMALES WANT TO BE RESCUED AND CONTROLLED.

Integrity demonstrates self-respect.

At the heart of being a godly guy is the quality of *integrity*. Someone once defined integrity as "living in the same manner privately as you do publicly." I like that definition but prefer the one that says: *Integrity is what you're like when no one is looking.*

key point
BE HONEST WITH YOURSELF.

When your son looks in the mirror, who does he see? Help him see inner qualities such as INTEGRITY as well as his outside appearance!

Integrity means that we are true to ourselves and honest with others. It means that we do the right thing simply because it is right. Your son needs to

Allows the Holy Spirit to work in and through us.

Shows respect for God and self.

INTEGRITY

Makes us more dependable.

Makes us even more reliant on God's grace.

realize that integrity is also being real with God. The adage "My word is my bond" is a statement of conviction and integrity. Point out to your son that most people can see through hypocrisy. Folks seem to intuitively know when we are wearing a mask. Keeping one's word and being honorable are signs of our true selves—they are active demonstrations of integrity.

Who are you when no one is looking? If parents are wearing masks to deal with others or their own kids, it provides a negative role model, and some guys feel that's permission to play the game as well. Integrity that is grounded in God's truth and grace will spill over to the football field, school classes, relationships with others, and family members. Remind your son that when Scripture commands us to approach God with clean hands and clean hearts, it is referring to *integrity*. Come clean. Be real. Be true to yourself and be honest. Honest to—and before—God!

BIG BIBLE POINT

Read and discuss these following verses about integrity with your son. Why do you think integrity is an important quality God desires us to have?

- Proverbs 10:9
- Proverbs 11:3
- Proverbs 13:6

SLIGHTLY OVER ONE-THIRD OF ADULTS (36%) ARE "SEARCHING FOR MEANING AND PURPOSE IN LIFE." WHAT DOES THIS SAY ABOUT HOW WE VIEW OUR LIVES?
(THE BARNA GROUP, 2001)

Discuss the following quote with your son and why it's good to be true to yourself and to God.

"This above all: To thine own self be true."
—*William Shakespeare*

Rick Bundschuh writes that "integrity is a trait that, if violated, demeans our claim to manhood." As parents, it's important to demonstrate integrity to our sons. Only then can we have the solid hope of our children rising up to be people of integrity.

Good character values others.

As boys grow into men, character becomes more important than charisma. Character is the molding and refining of a man. Words such as courage, persistence, care, and determination are words of character. It's important to teach your son that character values others and honors God.

Leaders put others first.

key point

LEADERS NEED TO BE POLISHED.

One of the ongoing debates in leadership circles is the question: Are leaders born or made? Are some born with God-given leadership traits, or does someone need to shape them in order for men to be leaders? I believe that leaders are both born *and* made. It takes a village to mold an individual. Some are definitely born with gifts and skills, whereas others are late bloomers. But all humans, no matter how gifted, need to be "polished" by God.

TARGET MOMENT

Discuss why being a leader means we're also able to be good followers. List other traits found in a good leader, including listening skills, compassion, and honesty.

Read Philippians 2:5-9. What attitude does Jesus have that we are to imitate? What does it mean that Jesus "humbled" himself? What can we learn about leadership from Jesus' attitudes and humility?

Nothing happens in a vacuum. A parent's primary purpose isn't to make children healthy, wealthy, and happy—it's to form and mold your child. Your mission is to help your son discover his giftedness and calling. This takes tons of time, patience, and endurance.

Developing your son into a leader means putting him in positions to grow. Speaking opportunities, student council, sports, mission trips, and service projects are all part of the ingredients that will forge a boy into a man—and eliminate Peter Pan's "I don't want to grow up" syndrome.

Leaders put others first.

Leaders respect others.

Leaders seek God.

Leaders follow Jesus.

Encourage your son to find ways to use his gifts and talents to lead others. Remind him that leadership begins with serving others!

One of your parental missions is to help your son value others. This is the start of leadership skills. Leaders put others first, and Jesus lowered himself to lift up others. He said the greatest people are those who serve instead of seeking to be served. Mark 2:1-12 tells us of four men who had a vision for one person. They carried a paralyzed man on a mat to be helped by Jesus. Jesus applauded the men's faith and vision. They saw a need and acted on it. Because of these men, the lame man would not only walk but leave a forgiven and free man. Let's teach our sons to lead, to see people's brokenness, and to reach out to them. *That* is leadership.

key point
LEADERS ACT OUT THEIR FAITH!

Courage means standing tall.

What does it look like to be strong? Is it simply a matter of muscles, or is there something more to strength? Is it a function of the physical or a trait of character? One of the developmental challenges for teenage boys is to figure out what it means to be strong.

key point

COURAGE IS MORE THAN BRAVADO.

The wise parent will help the male teen come to grips with the concept that true strength is rooted in *courage.*

Strength comes in many shapes and sizes. Remind your son that true strength is found in character and courage, not in muscles!

key point

PASSION & COURAGE ARE OFTEN RELATED!

Courage is more than bravado, which is an *arrogant defiance* or *reckless bravery.* If you look at many of the men in Scripture, they are not weak or just nice guys—but rather men with a passion. Can you imagine trying to lead over three million complaining Israelites as Moses did? Imagine having courage as Joshua had when he brought down the walls at Jericho! Imagine the courage of Paul, a newly converted Jewish Christian sharing his faith as people were ready to kill him. Biblical courage was much more than hollow bravado!

How can a teenage boy be courageous? One is in his convictions. Teen guys want to have a cause. They're torn between being popular, wanting people to like them, and having a vote of confidence from teachers, coaches, and mom and dad. So the pressure is on. A conviction is something a person believes in. I have seen boys stand courageously tall in the area of sexual purity. Some have bravely resisted the drug and party scene.

It takes courage to stand up for what you VALUE, what you BELIEVE in, and what you hold DEAR! Remind your teen that it's okay to say no!

HAVE **COURAGE** IN ...

1 Convictions

2 Abstinence

3 Defending others

4 Righting wrongs

Standing tall also means having the strength to stand up for what's right and to speak out against what is wrong. Courage comes in many shapes, voices, and forms. It always has a sense of honor, dignity, and concern for others.

Courage is defending and protecting a peer with "special needs" at the risk of being cast out of the high-school caste system. Others have stood to share their faith in class knowing verbal abuse would follow. Men, by nature, are protectors. I have seen grown men cry in order to defend children and babies. Teen boys can stand tall by befriending the loner at school, the kid who sits all alone in the cafeteria. Who will go sit with him?

"Courage is part of the fiber it takes to be a man."
—Rick Bundschuh

A spirit of serving serves us well.

key point
MODEL SERVICE TO YOUR SON.

Courage is not the only area in which to stand tall. A recent study revealed a troubling poverty and hunger level in America—even before Hurricane Katrina hit in 2005. The good news is that we can help the millions in need. Compassion is a sign of great character. When there is an enemy to defeat and a boy gets a vision to conquer it—whether it is a relationship, world hunger, poverty, diseases, or a child to tutor—guys can rise to the challenge!

key point
GUYS LIKE CHALLENGES TO SERVE AND HELP.

"Teaching boys to work is essential to preparing them for manhood."

—Dennis Prager

According to studies, more than 13 million children in the U.S. need food. Think of the ways your teen could help ease this need!

Why not serve lunch at a soup kitchen or collect canned goods for a local ministry or temporary housing units? Teach your son that we *are* capable of making a difference, then challenge him to seek ways to serve. Go to work with your son at a Habitat for Humanity home. It will inspire him—and you as well! Consider giving financially to Compassion International, which serves children overseas. Our sons will rise to the challenge if we will!

Discernment is another aspect of character development. One of the ways discernment emerges for adolescent boys is through working a job. It is while at work that a guy will learn what it means to be a man. Dostoevsky once said, "If you want to utterly crush a man, just give him work that's of a completely senseless, irrational nature." Guys are wired to work. Adam was to tend the land. A lot of our self-esteem and affirmation comes through getting a job and learning on the job. I believe it's good for teen guys to have part-time jobs while in high school. Work gives meaning to our existence and provides a good way to serve others.

Read aloud James 1:19 with your son. Then discuss how we can "serve with our ears," not just our hands. Remind your son that serving extends throughout our whole being and over-flows to God and others!

On the job, a teen will see other workers steal, cheat, be slackers, gossip, and perform with excellence. It will give him multiple opportunities to use his "sixth sense" to discern the right thing to do. Serving others requires discernment and wisdom—both of which can come from a job well done!

As your teen son discovers various ways to serve, he learns about giving of himself and how to manage life situations. Failures on the job are little intuitive messages to guys to "watch your back" because this could happen later in life with your marriage and raising your own children. Serving serves guys well.

BIG BIBLE POINT

"Each one should use whatever gift he has received to serve others, faithfully administering God's grace in its various forms" (1 Peter 4:10).

• How does serving others allow us to serve God?

• In what ways does service show honor to others?

• How can serving others help guys grow spiritually?

"Serve one another in love" (Galatians 5:13).

Good character values God.

Some of the main "spiritual" questions teen guys ask themselves are: *What do I really believe? Is there an afterlife? Does God exist? Are there many ways to know God? Who is Jesus?* Raising a teen with character will lead to a guy who values God—and is able to answer these questions in his heart!

Obedience begins with love.

A person with character is balanced and flexible. God did not create us like puppets that he can manipulate. He wants a relationship with us, so he gave us free will to love him or the choice to not respond at all. God will not force our hand for love. He demonstrates it all the time, but God will not trap us in order to choose love.

key point
LOVE IS A POWERFUL CHARACTER TRAIT!

Remind your teen that God created us with the sole purpose of connecting the creature (us) to the creator (God). We are wired for relationships on a vertical level with God and a horizontal level with people. Nothing else matters much, except the cultivation of character.

✔ Read 1 Corinthians 13 with your son.

✔ List the qualities of love on a sheet of poster board, then discuss how these help build character in our lives.

✔ Hang the list in a place to read often!

If you love someone, chances are you want to please that person. In a dating relationship, the guy who is crazy about a girl will do all kinds of things to prove his love. We will go out of our way to love, honor, and obey. The same is true for a guy who encounters the living, resurrected Jesus. When a guy is taken aback by the love of God, he will do anything. Jesus learned obedience to the ways of his Father, and so can we.

Teens are often caught up in the trap of performing for others, so they naturally think they need to earn God's love as well. Not true. We have been given a gift called "grace," which is God's riches at Christ's expense. When Jesus died courageously on that Roman gibbet, he was thinking of you and me. When I accept by faith that Jesus died for me and in my place, that is called *substitutionary atonement,* a big theological term for: *Jesus was my substitute!*

> He **humbled** himself and became **obedient** to death— even **death** on a **cross!**
> **(Philippians 2:8)**

> But **God** demonstrates his own **love** for us in this: **While** we were still **sinners**, **Christ** died for us.
> **(Romans 5:8)**

It has been said that if Christ hadn't been nailed to the cross, his love would have held him there! Look for ways to help your son nurture love in his character as he remembers we love because God first loved us. Challenge him to express his love for God and others in his obedience, sacrifices, and respect. For as love builds in our lives, so does character!

Love is a virtue that is even greater than faith and hope, according to God's Word! Check out 1 Corinthians 13:13 with your teen son, then discuss the following questions about the power and character found in love.

♥ Why do you think love, as a character trait, is even more important than faith and hope?

♥ How does love form the basis for all other qualities of character?

♥ What would life be like without God's love or our own love for God and others?

Humility honors God.

There is nothing quite like a teenage guy fired up for God. When we know we are forgiven for our sins, it frees us. But if he's not careful, a teen's excitement and confidence can lead to a proud spirit. Humility has been described as the way we bow before God—in giving God the glory and the credit for the blessings in our lives and for the good we accomplish. Being humble isn't always easy—it can be a challenge always to put others first and to keep our pride in check! But teen guys need to understand that it's only by and through God's gifts and grace that they are who they are!

key point
HUMILITY MEANS GIVING GOD THE CREDIT.

Remind your teen that winners turn into losers when they're not humble or forget to give God and others credit.

There has been a massive amount of work written about the Lord Jesus, but very little deals with his human-ness. He was the co-creator of the universe, says the book of Colos-sians. He will come back again as the conquering King. But while on earth, he was also fully human. Jesus cried, felt hurt, laughed, bled, slept, and ate. He learned obedience—and he demonstrated humility.

Discuss this quote with your teen and what it teaches us about humility.

"Every man is my superior that I may learn from him."
—Thomas Carlyle

So how does having a spirit of humility help teen guys? Humility places the glory back on God, where it belongs. Your son needs to realize that God is the giver of all good gifts and that God deserves the credit. Humility teaches guys to place others and their needs before them. It encourages a spirit of serving and sacrifice. Humility enhances relationships with girls. Most girls don't enjoy bravado or ego—and being humble shows that a guy's heart is clean, selfless, and ready to give to others.

Psalm 18:27

Psalm 149:4

How will God treat the humble?

Psalm 25:9

Psalm 147:6

In today's world, humility has gotten a bad rap. Humility doesn't mean thinking we're losers. Remember that your son is created in the image of God! Humility is a realistic appraisal of who you are from top to bottom. A humble person can identify his own strengths and weaknesses. God gives grace to the humble and detests the proud. People who exalt themselves—or debase themselves—are not humble. Philippians 2 tells us that Jesus was so humble that he denied himself to die for humanity so we could have eternal life. What a price Jesus paid through humility—and what blessings come to our sons through their own humility!

> **THE INTERESTING THING ABOUT HUMILITY IS THAT ONCE YOU THINK YOU HAVE IT, YOU PROBABLY DON'T!**

Seek and grow in God's wisdom.

key point
TRUE WISDOM COMES FROM GOD.

key point
WISDOM IS HEART & HEAD PUT TOGETHER!

As a 12-year-old, Jesus went to the temple and asked questions of the rabbis, or teachers. Luke 2:52 tells us that Jesus grew in both maturity and wisdom. Think about it. *Jesus grew in wisdom.* Even Jesus sought to gain wisdom to accomplish God's will in his life! So how do we teach our sons to make wise decisions and good choices? One insight from Luke 2 is that Mary and Joseph did not try to control Jesus (kind of hard to stop God!). Let your son learn the hard way by falling into some of life's ditches. Our hope is that our guys will develop an inner monitor that allows them to listen to the Holy Spirit—and gain wisdom.

BIG BIBLE POINT

Read aloud Hebrews 12:5-11 with your teen. Then discuss these questions.

- How does discipline guide your decisions and actions?

- What if there was no punishment or discipline in life?

- How are wisdom and discipline related?

- How can discipline help you be more obedient to God?

Wise parents seek God to guide their teen sons— not to control them!

As parents, we want to see our sons grow in wisdom, just as Jesus did. We pray for God's will to be done in our boys' lives. We let go of control and ask God to take control of our guys. They are really on loan from God anyway. God is really the parent, and we are just the overseers.

One of the ways we can teach wisdom to guys is through consequences. There are two kinds of consequences: *natural* and *logical.* Natural consequences are ones like gravity—you jump, you fall. If you run your car into a tree, the car is messed up and you may be hurt. Logical consequences are ones set up by you ahead of time, so that if a violation occurs, there are guidelines in place to teach guys how to respond. Consequences, by their very nature, help teens learn humility. The penalty should be related to the "crime." For example, breaking curfew with the car might mean a loss of the car for a few days.

Wisdom often comes from making mistakes and pressing limits. Be patient! Your son is learning important life lessons.

PARENT POINTS TO PONDER

❶ **What can you do if you don't like your son's friends?**

❷ **What boundaries can you help your son set concerning temptation and peer pressure?**

❸ **What are ways to be a friend to your son's friends?**

❹ **What are possible pluses and minuses of helping guide your son's choice of friends?**

Guys need clear-cut boundaries for behavior and consequences!

Spell out the losses or consequences that could occur for breaking curfew, a drop in grades, and behaviors you feel are inappropriate. Pose a united front, if you're married. Issues like drinking and driving or drug use could lead to loss of the phone, time with friends, or certain privileges and freedoms. Don't have unrealistic expectations or make unrealistic punishments ("You're grounded until you're 25!"). Put rules and consequences in writing, and you'll have a document to deal with infringements.

Acknowledge God with words and actions.

Jesus was a man's man! He was tough yet tender, wise, discerning, compassionate, and no wimp. He was strong on the outside and strong on the inside. Jesus knew when to be with people and when to be alone. He knew when to meet people's needs and when to head for the mountains for solitude and silence. Jesus was a man of faith. He leaned on his Father and praised God with his words and his lifestyle.

key point
LET YOUR FAITH FLOW NATURALLY!

key point
EXPRESS YOUR FAITH IN WORDS & ACTIONS.

Parents must serve God intimately if there is any expectation of their sons walking in the faith. There is no such thing as failure when it comes to walking with God—just trial and error. Assure your teen that it takes time to figure out how to live the Christian faith so that we constantly acknowledge God in all we say and do. Acknowledge God daily in prayer and action to provide a role model for your son.

" In **all** your ways **acknowledge** him, and **he** will **make** your **paths straight.** "

(Proverbs 3:6)

What would it look like for your family to talk about God for one week intentionally? Share Deuteronomy 6:4-8. Then set a goal to acknowledge God for one week as you wake up, go to bed, walk, and sit down.

Faith, and putting our faith into action, needs to be integrated into a parent's life—not just compartmentalized for Sundays. Teens can smell hypocrisy a million miles away! Does your son really pick up on times you model faith in action? You bet he does! Even if you are modeling behavior and not using words, your teen will know. Remember that over 75 percent of communication is nonverbal—and your own faith is communicated through your unspoken actions as powerfully as through your words.

Adults who attended church as a child or teen are twice as likely as others to...

Didn't go to church | Did go to church as teens
Read the Bible

Didn't go to church | Did go to church as teens
Pray to God

Attending church regularly can help your teen son learn to acknowledge God in his words and actions throughout the week. Worshiping *does* make a difference!

Faith, if fully modeled, must be natural, if teens are to want what we have. Help your son realize that his faith should influence and impact all areas of his life—from money and how it's spent to how he relates to his parents and neighbors. The ultimate goal is to pass on to our sons the spiritual torch that acknowledges God's power and presence in our lives. This is a generational legacy we're giving to our kids—and one that will last their whole lives through!

Read aloud James 2:22 with your son. Then discuss how acknowledging God in all we say and do is an example of putting faith into action. Discuss ways to put your son's faith into action this week.

Dangers & Snares

The Bible speaks of the many dangers that humans face. Teens on their way to manhood will quickly learn the battles that lie ahead. In the garden, temptation reared its ugly head, disguised as a snake. This serpent, known as the devil and the deceiver, has a plan to usurp and sabotage God's people—and teens are not immune to the dangers!

Tame teenage temptations.

Satan has a goal: to steal, kill, and destroy any goodness in people. His target practice: keeping boys from becoming men of God. His method: temptation!

Learn to flee the snake of temptation.

The snake is alive and continues to battle humans. Our culture hasn't helped either, with its proliferation of sexual ads, TV shows, videos, and DVDs, as well as Internet pornography.

key point
SEXUAL TEMPTATIONS ARE EVERYWHERE.

Until they're 9 or 10, guys think girls have "cooties." No one is sure what cooties are, but boys want nothing to do with girls until around middle school. Then there is a chemical within guys that produces pounding of the heart, sweaty palms, and even uneasiness in the stomach. When a guy likes a girl, it increases his intensity to win her over!

Boys begin to really notice girls in middle school!

Guys are physically wired like hydraulic engines that move fast! It takes men little to no time to sexually ignite and go into overdrive. Women's batteries take longer. Guys are turned on by sight—through the eye gate. Girls are stimulated much more by touch and affection. A guy can get aroused by just looking at a girl, a video, or a magazine.

key point
GUYS ARE VISUALLY STIMULATED.

key point
WE CAN OVERCOME TEMPTATIONS.

The power of sexuality cannot be minimized. Men and women throughout history have been destroyed by sexual temptations. Biblically, Samson was undone by his lust for Delilah, and David paid dearly for his affair with Bathsheba. But when Joseph was tempted by Potiphar's wife, he refused to give in to temptation. Joseph knew what was right and what was wrong—and chose to honor God by refusing to give in to his urges. Help your son understand that being tempted is not sin—but giving in may be!

Discuss the difference between love and lust with your teen son. Ask him how a guy can know if he's in love or simply "in lust." Share I Corinthians 13 with your son as you list the differences between love and lust.

"Part of the challenge Christians face in a lust-filled world is remembering that neither sex nor sexuality is our enemy. Lust is our enemy and has hijacked sexuality. We need to keep reminding ourselves that our goal is to rescue our sexuality from lust, so that we can experience it the way God intended."

Discuss the meaning of this quote from author Joshua Harris with your teen son. In what ways do you agree or disagree that sex is not the problem, but rather lust.

There's negative power in pornography!

At the click of a mouse, pornography can rear its ugly head on computer screens! Internet pornography is already growing at epidemic proportions. It only takes a short time for young males to discover soft- and hard-core pornography on their "user-friendly" computers.

key point
WEB PORN IS ONLY A SHORT CLICK AWAY!

> 89% of sexual solicitations are made in chat rooms or instant messages.
> (PEW study reported in *JAMA*, 2001)

Because guys are so visually stimulated, they can become addicted to looking at pornography in books, magazines, movies, or on the Internet. A sexy bathing suit will affect a guy every time! The guy is not so much turned on by nudity but by his imagination— a little cleavage can really stir his hormones! "Less is more" is often true to form with a guy when it comes to sexual thoughts about girls. The greatest sexual danger for a guy may be his own imagination and mind!

Although it's often easy for guys to blame girls for being objects of temptation, remind your son that the responsibility for resisting temptation and his own urges lies with him!

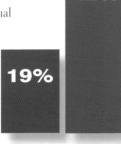

42%

19%

19% of Christians versus 42% of non-Christians said that whether or not it is acceptable to see pornographic videos or pictures is a matter of taste, not morality.
(Barna Group, 1997)

key point

GUYS MUST WORK AT RESISTING TEMPTATION.

Guys struggle with visual desire. That's why pornography can be so addictive. But we are sexual beings and made for intimacy within the context of marriage between a man and a woman. Premarital heterosexuality, extramarital sex, and homosexuality are warned of and forbidden by God. Remind your teen that although God loves people even when they do these things, he does not condone their actions. These sins can be forgiven and cleansed by God.

USE THE **PAUSE** BUTTON AND **TALK** TO YOUR TEEN!

T — **T** is for *time*. Spend quality time with your son—it speaks volumes to him!

A — **A** is for *affirm*. Make home a place for encouragement—not put-downs!

L — **L** is for *listen*. Focus on your son when he talks to you—he's worth it!

K — **K** is for *know*. Get to know your son's world—including his dreams, hopes, and fears!

Pornography is waging war against the souls of men. It starts quietly and secretively in the mind. It is progressive in nature and succumbs to the law of diminishing returns— the more you get, the more you want. It leaves men feeling guilty and shameful. Most males who are addicted hide it from others. If you are struggling with this addiction, get help. Overcoming pornography is not an easy battle to win—but you must fight for your son's protection. Take control of the Internet. Make a covenant to be a man of God, thinking about that which is honorable, pure, excellent, and admirable (Philippians 4:8).

REMIND YOUR SON TO...

"Watch and pray so that you will not fall into temptation. The spirit is willing, but the body is weak" (Matthew 26:41).

Beware of the "M" word—it's not marriage!

Most church youth ministries will deal with love, lust, sex, and marriage. But at all guy events, the "M" word will eventually come up—and guys get a little nervous when the leaders bring it up. Some have called it a "sumo-sex drive." We're speaking of masturbation, common to both genders. Most counselors agree that 99 percent of boys masturbate and that it's normal. The real issue is, What is driving the behavior when it gets out of control?

key point
GUYS NEED TO TALK ABOUT TEMPTATIONS.

The truth is, the Bible does not address the topic of masturbation. When you talk with your son, discuss that all guys have a sexual release in wet dreams. They happen while asleep and are natural, even normal. Many boys feel guilty over this experience and shouldn't. Whereas wet dreams are uncontrollable, the debate that emerges is whether *masturbation is controllable.*

key point
GUYS NEED TO FOCUS ON GOD.

There are many issues that may cause masturbation to become a real problem, including anxiety, nervousness, hidden anger, and feeling out of control in life. But perhaps one of the biggest issues surrounding this behavior comes from contact with pornography and a wandering mind and imagination.

Encourage your son to focus on being more like Jesus. This means focusing on faith, serving others, praying, and resisting temptations that draw him away from living as God desires him to live.

Author Joshua Harris says: "I think Christians make too big a deal of masturbation in that we obsess over the act and neglect the more important issues of the heart. God wants us to be more concerned with the soil of our hearts, out of which a lifestyle of masturbation grows. It's a mistake to make the act of masturbation the measure of our relationship with God" (from *Sex Is Not the Problem*).

Do you agree or disagree with this statement and why?

There are a number of ways to help your son overcome the issues that may be leading him into unhealthy behaviors. Authors Stephen Arterburn and Fred Stoeker, in their book *Every Man's Battle*, discuss how "bouncing your eyes" (moving them quickly away from temptations) is one way to avoid pornography and other visual stimuli that may cause a teen to stumble into masturbation. Another suggestion is to avoid sexually charged videos or music. Help your son find friends and mentors who will pray and hold each other accountable. And encourage your son to focus his life on Christ to help him avoid the pitfalls of obsessive behaviors.

Help your son avoid the traps of pornography, temptations, and masturbation by trying these simple suggestions.

- BOUNCE YOUR EYES
- AVOID SEXUAL IMAGES
- PRAY WITH A FRIEND
- FOCUS ON JESUS
- FIND A MENTOR
- SERVE & HELP OTHERS

51%

of Christians favor the idea of making it illegal to distribute movies or magazines that contain sexually explicit or pornographic pictures. (Barna Group, 1997)

There are roadblocks to manhood.

Girls commonly refer to males as unemotional. But males *are* emotional—the way information and feelings are processed is just different from girls. Let's look at guys and their emotions—and what roadblocks must be overcome for boys to grow into men.

Guys use "guy speak" to communicate.

Ask a teenage girl her opinion about adolescent guys, and you might hear comments such as: "Why can't they just say what they think?" or "What is up with the burps and noises?" or "How come he won't tell me what he is feeling?" Teenage girls intuitively know that teenage guys are less mature than they are. Immaturity often shows in guys' inability to articulate clearly and emotionally.

key point
GUYS MATURE MORE SLOWLY THAN GIRLS.

Guys and girls often have a communication gap— but that will change as guys mature into adults.

Our world is driven by words. And guess what? Women love the world of words—but most guys don't. Guys would rather be on a football field tackling some quarterback or watching a forward make the winning jump shot for the NBA finals. It's just that simple: *guys and words can be like oil and water!* Just observe teens at church. Who are normally the last to linger and chat? Answer: it's not the guys. They've left the building and are probably out running around!

DOING VERSUS FEELING: WHICH IS BETTER?

BOYS

Studies have found that 2-year-old boys are about three times more likely than girls to build a bridge out of blocks.

God made us as we are—and neither gender is better than the other!

GIRLS

Studies have found that 3-year-old girls can interpret facial expressions as well as or better than 5-year-old boys.

Guys follow guys. So we need strong, godly men whom boys can imitate. Guys don't follow programs; they follow men. Watch a TV talk show and look into the crowd. There are usually more women than men. Why? The topics deal with relationships. It's brilliant marketing, but men don't want to sit around and hear about weight loss and relationships. Guys are into doing. I wonder if the church, youth ministry, and schools need to rethink how to reach guys?

Author Gary Chapman describes five love languages:

- SERVICE
- QUALITY TIME
- PHYSICAL TOUCH
- GIFTS
- WORDS OF AFFECTION

Try and figure out what love language your son has and then focus on giving it to him. Don't stereotype. All guys don't fit the one-size-fits-all model here. Make sure that you don't push in an area that might not be his love language.

Keeping anger in check is important.

Anger is an emotion like any other feeling. The Bible tells us it's okay to be angry, but not to sin. Though it's normal to feel anger, there are good and bad ways of expressing it. "Blowing up" or clamming up are poor ways of handling anger and are common with many guys. It's sad, but most teenage guys don't know, or haven't even seen, healthy models of expressing their anger.

key point
ANGER IS A NATURAL EMOTION.

- breaking things
- verbal outbursts
- crying
- emotional shutdown
- talking with friends
- angry silence
- prayer
- retaliation

HOW DOES YOUR SON HANDLE HIS ANGER?

Discuss which of these techniques are healthy, which are poor, and why.

What does unhealthy anger look like? We tend to get angry over things that don't really matter, things that have no eternal difference. What about the guy who drives too slow? We go nuts with road rage. We get mad when our favorite football or basketball team loses. James 1:19 tells us to be slow to anger—but this can be a challenge for guys. Our teens will get angry at us, at friends, at school, with coaches and teachers. What are some of the hidden culprits that stir up guys' anger? Call it a *"Mess"*!

M Minimizing feelings

E Expectations too high

S Sarcasm from parents

S Shouting between people

What does nonsinful, appropriate anger look like? Jesus got angry, right? Since he never sinned, he must have had *righteous anger*. Jesus became mad at things like sin, injustice, people causing pain for others, and hypocrisy. Appropriate anger is directed at evil. We tend to get mad over insignificant things and not get angry over things that really matter.

Laws, social norms, and good old common sense tell us not to lash out physically or verbally every time something irritates us. Otherwise, we could hurt ourselves and others!

How do we help our boys keep their anger in check? Some questions we need to ask include: *Is my son battling low self-image? Are there family issues provoking the anger? What is happening at school that might be stressing him out? What relationships aren't working at school? Is he guilty about something? Does he feel mistreated?*

What is *reflective listening*? It is restating what someone says by reframing it in your own words. It can be in a question such as, "Am I sensing that you are mad at me?" or in a statement such as, "I hear you saying that not making the team really ticked you off."

How do we handle an angry guy? We can listen without being reactive. We can allow our guys to tell us exactly what they're angry about without judging them. As you listen, ask questions and then tell them what you heard them say. Finally, never argue with an angry teenager! It just makes matters worse. Punishing a boy for getting angry is rarely the best solution. Instead, love him and pray for him.

Guys often internalize their problems.

key point
GUYS PROCESS FEELINGS INTERNALLY.

key point
GUYS OFTEN HIDE THEIR PROBLEMS.

Though some girls think guys don't have any emotions, they do! Every male, just like every female, runs into disappointment, hurt, envy, pain, embarrassment, worry, despair, jealousy, joy, and anger. What happens to most girls is that they seem to be more "in touch" with their feelings. Estrogen helps girls cry and talk about their pain. Testosterone in guys seems to prevent emotional release and talking over experiences; it produces more of an internal, analytical approach.

Kids from fatherless homes are...

• 5 times likelier to commit suicide

• 32 times likelier to run away

• 20 times likelier to have behavioral disorders

• 9 times likelier to drop out of school

• 10 times likelier to abuse substances

(From *It's Better to Build Boys Than Mend Men*)

Because guys often have a difficult time expressing themselves, sharing emotions, and admitting problems, they may become despondent, depressed, and even hopeless. Watch for signs of depression, including...

• changes in sleeping habits
• changes in eating habits
• severe mood swings
• prolonged silence
• hopelessness
• isolation
• suicidal thoughts

Many guys may not be able to identify or articulate moodiness or depression. It takes a wise parent to help a teen pinpoint what's going on inside. Too many questions will probably turn a guy off, so your job is to watch and observe if there are warning signs of depression that could lead to larger problems.

12 WARNING SIGNS OF SUICIDE

FEELINGS OF REJECTION	GIVING AWAY POSSESSIONS
OUTBURSTS OF ANGER	OBSESSION WITH DEATH
WITHDRAWAL FROM FAMILY	ONGOING ISOLATION
DEPRESSION, SADNESS	CHANGE OF SLEEPING HABITS
PROBLEMS AT SCHOOL	TALKING ABOUT SUICIDE
A LOSS IN RELATIONSHIPS	FAMILY TRAUMA OR CHANGE

According to Dr. Richard O'Connor, in the past 25 years the suicide rate for those between 15 and 24 has tripled and is now tied for the second most common cause of death among adolescents. It's important to realize that teen guys do hold in feelings and may internalize problems to the point of hopelessness. Though some of the signs may indicate a serious health problem, such as a chemical imbalance, seek help immediately with a doctor, psychologist, or professional counselor if you think your son is struggling with thoughts of suicide or self-harm.

Specific plans: Does he have a plan?

Lethal plans: Is his method lethal?

Availability of method: Does he have access to his intended means?

Proximity of helping resources: Will his plan put him out of reach?

THE *SLAP* MODEL FOR DETECTING SUICIDAL THOUGHTS

(Rich Van Pelt and Jim Hancock, *The Youth Worker's Guide to Helping Teenagers In Crisis*)

There are many pressures from peers.

Wise parents are aware of peer pressure for their sons. There are a number of concerns to be worried about. But there's also positive peer pressures. In this section, let's look at both positive and negative peer pressures and how they affect our sons.

Fitting in isn't always the perfect fit.

It's pretty normal for guys to follow and imitate someone. We are all creatures of habit, and parroting another person happens all the time. There was a bumper sticker that read: *Don't follow me, I'm lost.* Oftentimes, we guys follow other lost guys.

HERO OR ZERO?

Guys are testing whether their parents have been honest with them. Be sure you're modeling the kind of choices and behavior you want your son to grow in his own life!

Encourage your son by:

- **Letting him** explore **new ideas and areas**
- **Allowing him to be** adventurous
- **Finding out what he's** good **at**

In Romans 12:2 we're told not to copy the customs and behaviors of this world. It's hard not to follow people and what they do. One of the main challenges we face is in helping our boys be self-differentiated. That means being able to say, "I don't want to do that," when everyone else is saying, "But we're going to." Boys are trying to decide whether they believe what we've taught them is true or false—whether parents are heroes or zeroes.

As boys continue in the process of becoming men, they'll start figuring out their self-image needs and their *identity wounds*. All boys get wounded, says author John Eldredge. And with wounds from the past, poor decisions, and present crises, a boy will either turn inward and fight the battle alone or come out and play the game. Every boy will hit some kind of wall of crisis and trouble.

Peer pressures include drinking, doing drugs, premarital sex, and pornography. Help your son understand it's okay to refuse.

key point

GUYS MUST FIGHT THEIR OWN BATTLES.

Feelings of inadequacy will eventually emerge. It will be at this stage that guys decide to put up or shut up. The pressure to drink, to do drugs, to have premarital sex will come. Guys don't think of the future ramifications of certain decisions and generally don't put into the mix what their parents will think.

"Films reflect our fantasies. Men fantasize about saving the world against impossible odds. Women fantasize about having a relationship with a wonderful man."
—**David Murrow**

A loving, caring parent will be able to see the landscape of where his teen is heading. You can pray, talk, and listen—but you cannot fight the battle for him. You must choose to let your son go into the war zone by himself or with a band of brothers. Unfortunately, young men who want to follow Christ don't see many peers desiring God, so it makes living the faith that much harder. A teen needs at least one "soul brother." Who will fight for the soul of your son? Pray for God to bring along a soul brother to help your son resist peer pressures.

Deal with fears of friends and failure.

key point
GUYS WORRY ABOUT MEASURING UP.

One of the most common fears for a teenage boy is the fear of saying no. Guys want to be cool and popular at times. And yet there is a guiding principle almost every guy values (whether he acts on it or not)—being true to himself. Guys almost universally dislike themselves when they compromise a value they hold up before others.

key point
IT'S HARD FOR GUYS TO STAND ALONE.

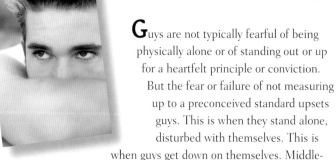

"Don't **fear** failure so **much** that you **refuse** to try **new** things. The **saddest** summary of a **life** contains three descriptions: **could** have, **might** have, and **should** have."

—Louis E. Boone

Guys are not typically fearful of being physically alone or of standing out or up for a heartfelt principle or conviction. But the fear or failure of not measuring up to a preconceived standard upsets guys. This is when they stand alone, disturbed with themselves. This is when guys get down on themselves. Middle-school and high-school boys hate not keeping true to what they intend to do. They feel alone because they feel as if they've let themselves—and others—down.

key point

CHOOSE YOUR FRIENDS WISELY.

Guys aren't typically people pleasers—but they want to be there for their friends. Scripture warns us that bad company corrupts good character, so guys need to be careful of the friends they choose. Friendships are about being cared for and about being accepted as we are, not about worrying if we measure up in some way. It is human nature to want others to like us—but guys need to use wisdom in choosing friends who won't lead them astray.

FRIENDLY TIPS FOR TEEN FRIENDS

❶ Teens can benefit from even the most ill-advised friendships. Sometimes the only way to learn how to choose good friends is to have a few bad ones along the way.

❷ When parents try to micromanage their teen's life, they rarely do better. Picking your sons friends is micromanaging at its worst.

❸ It's nearly impossible to force a teen to have the friends you want him to have.

❹ The only time to interfere with a teen's choice of friends is to protect him from serious and imminent harm.

(Wayne Rice, *Help! There's a Teenager in My House*)

What does this quote mean for guys who are afraid of measuring up?

"The young think that failure is the Siberian end of the line, banishment from all the living, and tend to do what I then did—which was to hide."
—James A. Baldwin

Parents may be able to set up guidelines for their sons' friendships—but they can't choose friends for them. Hopefully, our sons will choose wisely and see the wisdom in having friends who are solid and loyal and who make good decisions of their own!

TEEN TALK STARTER
"A real friend is someone who does not give you expectations about delivering on some kind of peer group pressure."
—Tony Orlando

Deal with gangs, gays, and "Goliaths."

Now for the toughest stuff of all. These are the three "biggies" that no parent wants to face—and all parents need loads of patience and understanding to deal with!

key point
BIG PROBLEMS NEED BIG PATIENCE!

1 What if my son has found new friends in a gang?

2 What if my son tells me he's gay?

3 What if there's a giant problem in some other area?

If your son has gotten into a gang, you cannot force him to get out, but you can perhaps alter the environment. Many gangs destroy individual freedom—forcing members to do and say as the gang dictates. If the gang majors in violence, you'll need to consider all options to protect your son. Sometimes it involves a geographical move from the gang. You cannot choose your son's friends, but you can surround him with other positive role models.

Teens often like getting a reaction from parents about the choice of their new-found "club" or gang.

Homosexuality is becoming more acceptable in American society, among teens as well as adults. The Bible teaches that homosexuality is contrary to God's design for men and women (Romans 1:18-27). It is clear that both men and women need nurturing from members of their own gender, but God's plan was for men and women to marry and share sexual intimacy.

TARGET MOMENT

Exodus International helps people trying to be free from the homosexual lifestyle. They can be reached at 888-264-0877 or at www.exodus-international.org.

Teen guys are dealing with the insecurities of sexual awareness, sexual-social functioning, and increased identification with male models not only in

> **"The bottom line is that homosexuality is not primarily about sex. It is about everything else, including loneliness, rejection, affirmation, intimacy, identity, relationships, parenting, self-hatred, gender confusion, and a search for belonging"** (James Dobson, *Bringing Up Boys*).

their families but in sports and team activities. This identification is important for a teen guy's security, self-esteem, and self-identity. It's not unusual for teen guys to wonder if they have homosexual tendencies—but this can lead to becoming convinced they truly are homosexual. Assure your son that just because he may wonder doesn't mean that he is.

key point

TREAT YOUR TEEN AS JESUS WOULD.

If your son has already fully embraced a homosexual lifestyle, or if you and your son are facing any other "Goliath" of a problem, you will want to find ways to cope and get support. It's critical to let your son know he is loved and accepted by you as a person even though you don't support his choice. Treat your son as Jesus would, neither condemning nor acquiescing to a lifestyle contrary to God's Word.

Some teens seek dangerous escapes.

We live in a world of addictions, habits, and dysfunctional patterns. Teens are not the only ones choosing addictions as dangerous escapes. Adults have also modeled abuses of sex, drugs, alcohol, and other behaviors and substances. It's important to deal with addictive behaviors in teens before they become adults and carry on dangerous habits for a lifetime!

Hopelessness can become "copelessness."

Depending on one's perspective, "acting out" started with the fall of man in Genesis 3. And Romans 3:23 makes it clear that we've all sinned and fallen short of God's glory. Nobody has his life together completely. Every human escapes into something, whether it's reading, TV, the Internet, cell phones, drugs, alcohol, work, or food. Some escapes appear harmless, whereas others have serious implications with negative effects on family relationships and society.

key point
WE ALL HAVE SOME NEGATIVE PATTERNS.

PAIN BY THE NUMBERS

95% of juvenile homicides are committed by boys.

80% of crimes that end up in juvenile court are committed by boys.

20% of violent crimes are committed by boys under 18.

Many of these boys come from broken or disturbed homes. Pain, hurt, and bad peers can turn teens toward lives of addiction, violence, and crime.

Youth leaders often believe that teens turn to negative behaviors out of curiosity. Christian and political leaders often attribute it to a decline in morality. Perhaps there is another room with a view. How about teens "behaving badly" because of pain and problems in their homes and hearts?

Teen guys and girls both deal with many situations at home—sometimes in addictive ways. Look for ways to support, encourage, and communicate with your teen!

Teens with tough family situations may feel depressed, hopeless, and confined—and turn to drugs, alcohol, or other dysfunctional behaviors as an escape. Haven't you heard of teens smoking pot or drinking, only to discover their parents were filing for divorce? Domestic violence or sexual abuse may be going on at home, so the teen starts popping pills to handle the insanity. Many teens might be the scapegoat only because they're trying to escape what they perceive is a hopeless situation. Their hopelessness has turned into "copelessness."

Murray Bowen, founder of Family Systems, states that habits or patterns pass from families in a generational legacy. Consider doing a family tree, called a *genogram*, to help your teen recognize past familial addictions. It could help prevent future sins for your son. (See the book *Genograms,* by Monica McGoldrick.)

According to *The Weekly Reader* National Survey on Drugs and Alcohol, 31% of kids in grades four through six say they've been pressured to try marijuana!

If your son is behaving badly, ask yourself why. Be ruthlessly honest with yourself. If you're married, bring it all to the table. Discuss what is happening in your family system that could be pushing your son off the cliff. If you're a single parent, seek out support. Remember that no one is an island unless he chooses to be. If there is tension in the home, teens will escape in many ways—and some of them could be life-threatening!

Drugs make people dopey.

We've been told for years that drugs are painkillers. Well, they might kill pain for some, but they will eventually destroy lives as well. I have never heard a former drug addict expressing joy at having used drugs. I am one who experimented with drugs and alcohol in high school. I made some poor choices and am glad I'm no longer in bondage to drug usage. I have been forgiven for my past, but I'm not proud of what I used to do. It's true: *Drugs make people dopey.*

6 KEY CATEGORIES

- Cannabis (marijuana)
- Stimulants (methamphetamines, cocaine)
- Depressants (alcohol, barbiturates, tranquilizers)
- Narcotics (opium, heroin, morphine, codeine)
- Hallucinogens (PCP, LSD)
- Inhalants (nitrous oxide, chlorohydrocarbons, etc.)

Good news! While hallucinogens are popular, less than 15% of all teenagers are addicted to them.

So if drugs can destroy lives, distort decision making, become so addictive, and even kill the person taking them, why do so many teens choose to use? For many reasons, including: personal pain, peer pressure, popularity, escape, depression, and curiosity. With so many drugs to deal with, parents need to be aware of the types and their effects. The most popular chemical choices for today's teens to abuse include *marijuana*, *methamphetamines* ("meth"), and *inhalants*.

"The measure of a parent is not when all is well, but rather, how you stand when hardships and struggles are present."

Mark Gregston (Heartlight Ministries)

If you want to model abstinence concerning drugs, then are you practicing what you're preaching? If you don't want your son to smoke or drink, then you shouldn't either, correct? We can't say "don't" if we "do." Be as consistent as possible in your lifestyle. Surround your teen with alternative ways to have fun, and help him have coping skills when times aren't so fun. If your son gets involved with the drug scene, process with him the dangers and consequences. Help him figure out how to get out of the ditch.

In the next 24 hours, over 15,000 American teenagers will try drugs for the first time!

BIG BIBLE POINT

Share Luke 10:27 with your son. Discuss how drugs keep us from obeying this verse. List things drugs prevent people from doing or enjoying in their lives. Pray for strength to resist drugs.

According to Dr. Harold Voth, five marijuana cigarettes have the same cancer-causing capacity as 112 conventional cigarettes. Continuous marijuana usage over time will retard the part of the brain that allows persons to concentrate, create, and learn conceptually. Those who smoked one marijuana joint every other day for a year had a white blood cell count that was 39% lower than normal, damaging the immune system and making the user susceptible to infections and sickness.
(Harold Voth, *How to Save Your Kids From Drugs*)

If you sense a problem but your son denies it, take him to a medical doctor or drug counselor to be tested. Many times kids who are addicted need more than church and prayer— they need a facility with professionals who can monitor, coach, and advise in an objective environment.

Alcohol kills your perspective.

Alcohol kills off brain cells, therefore killing our perspective and good decision-making skills. Drinking damages the brain's chances to grow normally and affects the teen's mental and emotional health. Not only is drinking unhealthy for the body and mind; adolescence is the worst time to use alcohol.

key point

ALCOHOL DESTROYS BRAINS & LIVES!

The number one substance abused by today's preteens and teens is alcohol. Studies have shown that nearly four million Americans under the age of 18 are alcoholics!

The average age American teens begin drinking regularly is about 15 years.

Most alcoholics start early—some beginning as young as 10 years old! Those who choose to abstain during the teen years have a greater success rate of drinking responsibly—or not at all—as an adult. Studies have also suggested that alcoholism is a family-systems "sin," creating a genetic disposition. If there is a generational pattern of drinking and alcoholism in your family, the warning signs are there for your son—and for you to be aware of.

Those who experiment with alcohol shouldn't be considered the same as those who regularly use or are addicted ... but still take precautions! *Every alcoholic started by experimenting!*

"A child who reaches age 21 without smoking, abusing alcohol, or using drugs is virtually certain never to do so." — Joseph A. Califano Jr.

Does the Bible say anything against drinking and drugs? Scripture doesn't say not to drink—but it does warn against drunkenness. God tells us that our bodies are to be indwelt with his Spirit, to be led and controlled by the Holy Spirit. Alcohol and other destructive substances cause us to lose control and harm our bodies.

It is more important to ask the questions: *Does alcohol (or drugs) glorify God? Does it make me dependent on God or the drug?* We all know the real answer to those questions. Alcohol skews our perspective. It opens the door to lack of judgment and overall loss of wisdom.

BIG BIBLE POINT

Share 1 Timothy 4:12 with your son, then discuss how living as a good example of Christ's love provides all the hope we need—without using chemicals or addictive behaviors.

key point
DRINKING DOESN'T GLORIFY GOD.

Various studies have shown that families that eat even one meal together each day have a greater level of trust and communication. Make it a point to share meals—and yourselves!

Another important danger of drinking under the age of 18 in most American cities and states is that it's illegal. If a teen is picked up for drinking and driving, it goes on his driving record—and stays there for a long time! Remind your son that drinking and driving is a recipe for disaster at the least—and death at the worst!

Every weekend, nearly 40% of American teens will use drugs and alcohol. Will your son be one of them?

Forming Real Relationships

The relationships that influence teens the most are the nuclear family, extended family, adult relationships, and peer friendships. There are systems in life that drive boys to be open or closed relationally.

Friendships need strong foundations.

Family systems teach that the whole is greater than the sum of the parts. We know that all normal, healthy relationships will have conflict. The question is, how will we handle it? The heart of relationships is determining the way to be open or closed through effective communication.

Personality traits affect relationships.

We've seen that God created us male and female. But all of us have parts of the other in small ways. We all share certain qualities even if we have separate genders. It's okay for guys to cry or be nurses, and it's okay for girls to be race-car drivers or strong athletes. Each person on the planet is wonderfully and fearfully made by God. Guys have some feminine characteristics, and girls have some masculine qualities. But we all have personalities and must learn how to mesh those personality traits with a variety of people to get along.

key point
EVERYONE HAS UNIQUE PERSONALITY TRAITS.

We laugh at stereotypes—but remember that not all guys are quiet, nor are all girls gossips. Not all males are insensitive, not all girls emotional. No one size fits all teenagers. Saying that, we need to ascertain that many guys are somewhat of a challenge when it comes to being open in relationships. One of the fundamental issues is with temperament.

The Kiersey-Bates personality inventory lists four paired personality types that affect our relationships with others.

KIERSEY-BATES INVENTORY LIST
What kind of personality traits does your son have?

EXTROVERT / INTROVERT	**Extroverts are driven by the outside world, desiring to be around people. Introverts are driven by solitude.**
THINKER/ FEELER	**The Feeler makes decisions on his hunches, emotions, and values. The Thinker bases his on logic.**
SENSATE/ INTUITIVE	**A Sensate uses the senses to take in information. The Intuitive person goes with his gut instincts.**
JUDGING/ PERCEIVING	**The Judging personality loves closure and deadlines. A Perceiving personality craves spontaneity and open-endedness.**

Remember: one's not right or better—we're just different!

Most teenage guys, in temperament studies across the board, lean toward the Introvert and Thinker sides. They want logic—not emotion. They desire to go on gut feelings instead of their senses. It's no wonder girls and guys often have trouble communicating and meshing in their relationships!

Families affect relationships.

key point

FAMILIES CAN AFFECT OUR RELATIONSHIPS.

There are different family systems that provide a sense of openness or closeness for our sons that are then carried into other relationships. Parents cannot be ostrich-like, hoping that certain patterns will not exist or go away. Let's explore these family systems and how they affect our sons' ability to form relationships—or to avoid them.

RIGID SYSTEM

A RIGID family system operates with one authoritarian leader. The way to survive this system is to submit or run. It's often legalistic, with the leader's motto being: *My way or the highway.* The rigid system is high on rules and low on relationships. If a teen hates this system, he may comply, but only out of fear. This dictatorship can cause a teen to seek control in other relationships.
The result: battle with low self-esteem, performance-driven love, and depression

CHAOTIC SYSTEM

The CHAOTIC system is high on relationships and low on rules. It operates impulsively, with no one sure who's in charge. Sometimes it is mom, or dad, or the kids. In this home, parents often want to be "friends" and not lead or set boundaries. Discipline is erratic and inconsistent. Intentions are well meaning with communication, but follow-through rarely happens. The chaotic family doesn't handle conflict—it just sweeps it under the carpet.
The result: role confusion for a teen's present and future relationships

DISENGAGED SYSTEM

In the DISENGAGED family system, members are emotionally disconnected. Their motto might well be: *Busyness is next to godliness.* This is perhaps the number one family system today. Family members are emotionally unglued—there's no time to eat together, they're constantly on the run, and there is little attachment but a lot of hurriedness. This system is closed to communication, and when problems arise, everyone scatters.

The result: creation of "lost" boys who can become lost men in lost relationships

CONSIDER THIS...

✦ What kind of family system did you come from?

✦ What system are you raising your son in now?

✦ How do family systems affect relationships outside of the home?

ENMESHED SYSTEM

The ENMESHED family system looks close-knit and well-bonded from the outside, but on the inside, the teens are saying, "Let me out of here! I'm drowning and suffocating!" This family system has overprotective parents who want to know every detail of their teen's life—and may violate their teen's privacy. This family has unhealthy closeness and enmeshment.

The result: a teen who rebounds in the opposite direction and may push people away in relationships

Dating sets the stage for romance.

The dating adventure often begins in middle school with today's teens, then becomes even more popular during high school. Oh, the joys for teens—and the prayers for parents! It's a wild ride filled with ups, downs, hurts, and happiness—and never a dull moment.

Meeting others makes you vulnerable.

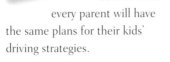

Author Tim Smith suggests that we consider dating like driving. Some states allow teens to get a temporary license around 15 years old. Under the supervision of the driving instructor, the state, and the parent, a driving test is taken. If the teen passes the test, he can drive. But guess who owns the car keys in most cases? It's up to the parent to determine the what, when, and where questions of driving. Just because the student has a license in hand doesn't mean every parent will have the same plans for their kids' driving strategies.

The Darker Side of Dating

Remind your son that girls can feel vulnerable on dates, and in fact, many rapes occur during dates. Discuss with your son that date rape is not about miscommunication or temptation. It's about guys who refuse to respect the feelings and boundaries of others.

PARENT POINTER

Parenting your first teenager when it comes time for dating can be more upsetting for us than for them! Before you start the dating drama, consider reading two books with two radically different approaches:

✦ *I Kissed Dating Goodbye*, by Joshua Harris

✦ *How to Get a Date Worth Keeping*, by Henry Cloud

Parents are the instructors in the game of dating. We teach and instruct our guys on how to meet girls, dating etiquette, what it means to be polite, opening doors, treating girls with respect, inviting a girl on a date, how to handle bad dates, and how to think of creative, fun places to go.

Have a day in which you discuss and plan out dating strategies. Dating is risky, like driving, so age is not the issue—maturity is. Dating confidence is one area parents can help with!

Guys need preparation before dating! They'll not learn much from their friends except bad habits. They need to know that dating is to be fun, not serious. It is not about finding "Mrs. Right" in the high-school years. It is about discovering life, enjoying other people, and learning a whole lot about themselves. Guys need to know the good, bad, and ugly sides of dating.

When should he date?

How can he meet girls? How should he treat girls?

Should he date in a group or one on one?

What might he wear?

What are some places he could take a date?

How can he talk respectfully with her parents?

What fears and concerns does he have?

Guys also need to hear from men and women alike about respect, politeness, and valuing others. Though dating can seem a bit like driving, remind your son that the girls he dates are created in God's image—and are not just metal objects like cars! Relationships are God's gifts to us—and dating is a fun part of relating!

Be creative in your together times.

key point
PREPARE FOR FUN DATES AHEAD OF TIME!

God's Word doesn't mention dating or courtship. In fact, many biblical relationships were arranged by parents. It makes some sense that parents would set up a match, because we have more wisdom, experience, and insight than our teens; plus, we think we know what our kid needs in a mate.

Even though the Bible is silent on dating, it's not silent on relationships with the opposite sex. There are guidelines on how to treat each other. We are to honor and respect each other and avoid the appearance of evil.

✓ **A BIT OF PREPARATION CAN REALLY HELP!**

SUGGEST AN ACTIVITY YOU'LL BOTH ENJOY.

The whole idea behind going out on a date is having fun. Nothing ruins this faster than choosing an activity that only one of you enjoys. Decide on something you both like, then plan your outing and time accordingly.

WHAT IS THE RIGHT AGE TO BEGIN DATING?
According to 13-year-olds in a recent study, most believe dating should begin in the early to mid teens!

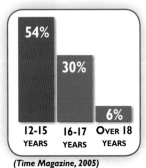

54%		
	30%	
		6%
12-15 YEARS	16-17 YEARS	OVER 18 YEARS

(Time Magazine, 2005)

Isn't dating meant to be creative, if done right? How do we encourage our kids to just have fun and not be pressured into sexual thoughts and perhaps even promiscuity? What boundaries can guys and girls set to protect themselves from a crash? All it takes is a little thought and preparation to find fun together times to share on a date and help steer clear of dating dangers.

In some schools, people date exclusively, while others just "go out" as friends. Some people hang out at coffee shops, sporting games, and parties. Help your son look for fun ways to share time with girls and to keep dating on the light, fun side!

DID YOU KNOW THAT...

About 60% of teens 16-17 don't date on a regular basis?

BEFORE YOU INVITE A GIRL ON A DATE, ASK YOURSELF...

- Does this person make me feel happy?
- Do we share any interests or hobbies?
- Does this person pressure me?
- Does this person make me laugh?

7 FUN DATES!

- ✦ Go canoeing, if your date likes water.
- ✦ Go Christmas caroling at a nursing home in August. Don't forget the candy canes!
- ✦ Go hiking and collect stones, leaves, or wildflowers.
- ✦ Watch a kids' soccer or baseball game.
- ✦ Visit an art museum, then paint pictures.
- ✦ Take a picnic to the park and play on the swings and slides.
- ✦ Go skating or bowling with a group of friends.

TEEN TALK STARTER

Joshua Harris's book, *I Kissed Dating Goodbye,* focuses on the concept of *courtship.* In this book, courtship is defined as a "relationship between a man and a woman who are actively and intentionally together to consider marriage." Discuss the differences between dating and courtship with your teen. Remind him that dating doesn't mean that you want to marry that person—it means having fun meeting others, learning about yourself, and *may* lead to courtship in the future.

There's no need to get too serious too soon!

Dating for many guys can turn into a serious enterprise. A lot of guys and girls in high school are dating one person to the exclusion of all others. But reminding your son that dating doesn't have to be—nor probably should be—too serious can relieve some of the pressures of dating. Guys need to remember that the reason behind dating is to get to know a girl better—not to get too serious or to think about marriage.

key point
KEEP DATING IN PERSPECTIVE!

Dating can be nerve-wracking for guys and girls alike. Make it easier for your son by offering advice and a listening ear!

"Most of the **girls** I go out with are just good **friends.** Just because I **go out** to the cinema with a girl, it doesn't **mean** we are **dating."**
—**Leonardo DiCaprio**

Some high-school sweethearts will marry, but they are in the minority. Dating might be a classroom for marriage with college-aged young adults, but in high school your son should consider it more like a playing field for maturing and understanding the opposite sex.

Before your son asks a girl out, ask these questions to make sure he's ready for dating and relating. If he cannot answer adequately, then he may not be ready to date yet.

❖ **Why do you want to date "this" girl?**

❖ **What attracts you to her?**

❖ **How can you handle sexual urges you might feel?**

Dating Tips for Guys

Dating is a complicated and confusing process—and can strike fear and anxiety in the hearts of guys everywhere! The three key steps to a date include inviting the right girl, deciding what to do, and ending the date in a friendly fashion. Here are a few tips and hints to help your son enjoy his dating experience—and grow in the process!

 TIP #1 A good date should consist of meaningful conversation. Sharing a meal is a great way to relax and get to know somebody!

TIP #2 Avoid being totally alone with your date. Recognize that girls might feel threatened or uneasy when alone with a person they hardly know—and sexual temptations may become too great for both guys and girls!

TIP #3 Decide in advance who will pay or if you'll go "dutch." Guys need to be sure to bring enough cash for both just in case.

TIP #4 Even though it might seem fun, good-night kisses should be avoided on a first date. Choose a handshake or quick hug instead.

 TIP #5 "I had a wonderful time" should be stated only if these are the guy's true feelings. If he had a lousy time, he should still be respectful of the girl's feelings and speak in a polite manner. Whatever the case, a guy should always thank the girl for spending time with him.

Abstinence before marriage is important!

The Bible is clear: sexual impurity is a sin—for everyone. And being sexually active before marriage creates many problems, from unwanted pregnancies to sexually transmitted diseases. The best way to prepare for marriage is to commit to sexual abstinence until the marriage day. Easier said than done, right?

In the movie *A League of Their Own,* Geena Davis plays Dot, the star catcher in this all-girls league. She's ready to quit and tells her manager, "It's just too hard!" The response from her manager? *"If it were easy, everybody would do it."* Teens need to understand that sex is fine—in the right context. And that context is marriage.

SEX IS G.R.E.A.T.

Share this acronym with your son to remind him that sex is much more than a mere physical act—and is meant for *marriage.*

GOOD (God saw all that he created was good.)

RELATIONAL (Sex is not just an "act." It's about two people who love each other.)

EMOTIONAL (What causes excitement *and* harm in relationships are the emotions of romance and sex.)

AFFIRMING (People want affirmation. Intimacy reveals so much about one another in every way, letting us know we're loved, trusted, and respected.)

TECTONIC (Sexual intimacy can create a powerful connection—but also can be devastating.)

Let your son know that it takes courage to go against the grain and not give in to sexual urges before marriage. Tell your boy it is easy to have sex before marriage—but it won't satisfy him or please God.

Check out the movement called *The Silver Ring Thing*. It is for both guys and girls, promotes sexual purity, and asks for a commitment to remaining abstinent until marriage.

Help your son come up with and sign a predating covenant containing specific dos and don'ts related to his actions, such as manners, etiquette, flirting, handling sexual urges, and so on. This could help keep him pure—and prevent regrets later in life!

Explain that guys who brag about their sexual encounters are at best exaggerating the truth—and at worst, full of shame, guilt, and disrespect. Tell your son that on his honeymoon he'll have great joy in knowing he saved himself for his wife. There will be mystery, great expectations, and no guilt or shame, no sexually transmitted diseases, and no unwanted pregnancy. Best of all, he'll have a clear conscience before God. Sexual intimacy is great, but waiting to enjoy the pleasures of intimacy in marriage is awesome!

BIG BIBLE POINT

Read Hebrews 13:4 and 1 Thessalonians 4:1-8 with your son. Then discuss these questions:

* How does one give honor in marriage?
* Why does God seem to be against sex before marriage?
* What does it mean to be holy?
* What does it mean to love another person?

DID YOU KNOW THAT...

* 50% of all STDs occur between the ages of 15 and 24.
* 4,000 deaths occur each year from HPV (sexually transmitted disease).
* 50% of sexually active Americans have genital warts.

Love is what it takes!

Dating, respect, abstinence—what does it take to make a solid, lifelong relationship work and flourish? 1 Corinthians 13 has the answer! It takes love—and loads of it! Help your teen son understand that love is the basis behind a strong marriage and a lifetime commitment.

Learn the levels of love.

key point
IT ALL BEGINS WITH LOVE!

Perhaps you didn't know this, but there is one book in the Bible that speaks almost entirely of love and sex. Do you know the name of the book? It's called *Song of Songs* or *Song of Solomon*. Some think it's an allegory of Jesus and the church, but it's actually a love song between a man and woman—and it's very sensual! In fact, Jewish boys could not read the Song until they reached a certain age!

The Greek concept of love is much deeper than simple mushy-gushy emotionalism. The Greek view is that love is threefold, according to the level of selflessness or personal payoff. *Philia* love is that of friendships, *eros* is physical love, and *agape* is selfless love of the highest form. Many marriages don't make it because one of these three ingredients is missing.

TEEN TALK STARTERS

Does your teen agree or disagree with these statements—and why?

1. Girls give sex to get love.
2. Guys give love to get sex.
3. God is forgiving if you've sexually blown it.
4. Oral sex isn't sex, so it's not wrong.
5. Premarital sex won't affect a relationship.
6. Guys and girls have different sexual standards.

LOVE TIMES 3

Discuss these forms of love from the Greek language with your son. Which love does he feel for the girls he dates and why? How is Christ's love for us a higher form of love and not dependent on the physical or on payoffs?

AGAPE	SPIRITUAL LOVE	This is Christ's all-accepting, selfless love for us. It's not self-serving but always puts others first. This is the love we're called to have.
PHILIA	EMOTIONAL LOVE	This is the love of friendship, but there is usually a payoff such as acceptance, friendship, and affirmation.
EROS	PHYSICAL LOVE	This is love of the body—physical love with a physical payoff. It's the lowest form of love, and some contend it is barely real love at all.

God created us as sexual beings meant to be in relationship with each other. Our sexuality is one of the ways we learn about ourselves, and it influences how we treat the opposite sex. Waiting until marriage to become intimate is a way to honor God's desires, to respect ourselves and our partners, and to help ensure the survival of an important, life-giving relationship! Before your teen is mature and ready to marry, he must understand that love is about applying selfless love and value in marriage. What's love got to do with it? *Everything!*

WHO HAS TRADITIONAL MORAL STANDARDS?

95% of Christians

86% of non-Christians

(Barna Group, 1997)

Marriage requires hard work!

Marriage was created by God and blessed by Jesus. It is a picture of how Jesus and the church work together. Marriage, as we spoke about it earlier, is finding the right woman and being the right man.

key point
MARRIAGE TAKES HARD WORK!

It is meant to be a fit. What many teens fail to realize is that marriage takes hard work to succeed. It begins with a man and a woman focused on God and sharing love and life—and is accomplished through patience, perseverance, prayer, and good old-fashioned work!

Discuss these quotes with your son. What do they teach us about marriage, its value, and the hard work involved?

"People try much less hard to make a marriage work than they used to fifty years ago. Divorce is easier."—Mary Wesley

"Where there's marriage without love, there will be love without marriage."—Benjamin Franklin.

"Don't marry the person you think you can live with; marry only the individual you think you can't live without."—James C. Dobson

Help your son realize that, when two people come together, there will naturally be differences and conflicts. Chances are, boys have seen good and bad marriages. Why is it so hard? Guys and girls are raised in different styles and places. Perhaps one is wealthy and the other poor. Maybe one was raised in an uptight home and the other in a more relaxed family atmosphere. Maybe one's parents knew how to communicate, and another grew up around anger. People are different—and people require patience.

Guys need to know that marriages take work. They'll need to work at listening, loving, connecting, managing finances, raising kids, and communicating. A dynamic marriage is a marriage worth waiting for and working at. In the meantime, here is some good advice for guys as they move closer to the time and person God has set aside for them.

1.

THERE IS NO REASON TO BE IMPULSIVE. **Take your time! If you want to have a great marriage, enjoy life. Consider college. Study hard. Work hard, play hard, and sleep hard. Play the field with respect and kindness.**

2.

MARRIAGE IS ORDAINED TO BE "TILL DEATH DO US PART." **Guys need to know that divorce is not a good option. Adultery is not an option. There are no back doors to leave the marriage. It is permanent. Leave your family and cleave to your spouse. The word** *cleave* **is from the Hebrew concept for glue, meaning that God wants to super-glue couples together so they don't separate.**

3.

PRAY—SEEK GOD'S WISDOM AND PLAN FOR YOU. **It is not easy meeting the "right one." In the meantime, work on making yourself the best you can be. Seek God and be patient. Pray for your future wife—whoever she might be. Wait for God's plan, and don't settle for second best.**

It takes courage to face the future!

As a teen grows into an adult, the number of challenges and choices he faces multiplies daily! Your son must ultimately take responsibility for the kind of person he becomes—and for the challenges and choices he embraces.

Choose to become a man of God.

FOR PARENTS

Will boys be boys? Hopefully not forever, for there is a lifetime of choices ahead of them as young adults growing into men. They may choose college, the military, or a vocation. They may choose to get married or remain single. They may or may not rise to the challenge of raising children. If you've raised your son to be dependent on God and self-reliant, you have done your job—and the challenges and choices are now up to your son.

Young adults must become responsible for their own challenges and choices!

FOR TEENS

A word to the young adult: Welcome to the new world called "growing up." Don't you hate that term? It is a scary world, but you love a challenge. Your purpose is to know God and make him known. You are called to make a difference in the world. It is now time for you to stand tall, figure out who you are and who you really want to be, and then go for the gold. As I left for college, I realized it was now "my time to pack my bags." What will you put in your bags? What tools of the trade will go in there? Will you survive or thrive? The choice is up to you. You decide today what tomorrow might bring.

The decisions you'll make in the future truly make a difference to God, the people you are with—and your own life, happiness, and faith.

Choose to be wise, discerning, and a man of your word. Choose to be a man of integrity and character. Let people see Christ in and through you as you venture forth to change the world!

key point

SEEK GOD IN ALL YOUR LIFE.

RISE TO THE CHALLENGE— MAKE THE CHOICE TO SERVE! Becoming a man of God means seeking ways to serve. At church, take the responsibility of finding ways to help, serve, and minister to others. Don't wait to be invited— rise to the challenge willingly!

Discuss these four aspects of becoming a godly man and how they will serve your son throughout his life. Why is it wise to choose each?

HONESTY Be true to God, to those you love, and to yourself. *(Proverbs 6:14)*

HUMILITY Put others before you and remember that God gets the glory! *(Proverbs 3:34)*

HOPE Face each day with joy, for God has plans for your tomorrows! *(Proverbs 23:18)*

HONOR Respect others, and you will honor God. *(Proverbs 19:17)*

Remind your son that the man he chooses to be will be his living testimony to God!

Show me the man you honor, and I will know what kind of man you are. —*Thomas Carlyle*

More Resources

BOOKS

for teens

- Shawn Covey, *Daily Reflections for Highly Effective Teens* (Fireside, 1999).
- Shawn Covey, *The 7 Habits of Highly Effective Teens* (Fireside, 1998).
- Pamela Espeland, *Life Lists for Teens: Tips, Steps, Hints, and How-Tos for Growing Up, Getting Along, Learning, and Having Fun* (FreeSpirit, 2003).
- Annie Fox and Elizabeth Verdick, *The Teen Survival Guide to Dating and Relating* (FreeSpirit, 2005).

for parents

- Stephen Arterburn and Fred Stoeker, *Every Man's Battle* (WaterBrook, 2002).
- Rick Bundschuh, *Passed Thru Fire* (Tyndale, 2003).
- Foster Cline and Jim Fay, *Parenting Teens With Love and Logic* (Pinion, 1990).
- James C. Dobson, *Bringing Up Boys* (Tyndale, 2001).
- John Eldredge, *Wild at Heart* (Thomas Nelson, 2001).
- Michael Gurian, *The Wonder of Boys* (Putnam, 1997).
- Joshua Harris, *Boy Meets Girl* (Multnomah, 2005).
- Crystal Kirgiss, *What's Up With Boys?* (Zondervan, 2004).
- Barbara and Allan Pease, *Why Men Don't Listen and Women Can't Read Maps* (Broadway Books, 1998).
- Wayne Rice, *Help! There's a Teenager in My House* (InterVarsity Press, 2005).
- Timothy Smith, *Connecting With Your Kids* (Bethany House, 2005).

WEBSITES

- www.lifeteen.org (resources and training that encourage teens to grow in their faith)
- www.christianteens.net (Christian chat, an online youth pastor, a teen message board, and much more)
- www.christianitytoday.com/teens: solid dating advice, help for living out your faith, articles about TV shows and movies, personal stories from other students, and recommendations for cool Christian music
- www.firepower.org (a site for connecting teens grades seven and up)
- www.streetdrugs.org (a wide-ranging resource with a guide to identifying drug use, a survey of drug laws, common "street" terms for drugs, and more)
- www.screenit.com/index1.html (reviews and suggestions for making wise entertainment choices)
- www.bebroken.com (an online leader in sexual-addiction resources, with an emphasis on promoting biblical purity)

Subpoint Index

Chapter 1: The Gift of Gender   8

Chapter 2: Qualities of a Godly Man   26

Chapter 3: Dangers & Snares 50

Chapter 4: Forming Real Relationships 74